WHAT DOES THIS COMPANY DO?

·

WHAT DOES THIS COMPANY DO?

Understanding a Business and its Risks

DRAGO DIMITROV, CFA

For my wife, Kelly.

CONTENTS

PREFACE

I assume you are either an investor or someone who wants to break into the investments industry. What attracts you to this profession?

Perhaps it's receiving the monetary reward of a successful investment, which can happen due to luck or application of a sound investment process over time. It could also be the recognition (both to the self and to others) that you are a competent decision maker in the face of uncertainty. Yet such a reputation can come through the misleading halo effect of successful outcomes, making its status fleeting. And on the basis of successful outcomes alone, you might always be gnawed by the thought of "What if I just got lucky? How do I know whether I truly have the skills of a great investor?"

Independent of outcomes, you can validate investment competence through the quality of thinking presented *a priori* before the investment decision. This is particularly important at the junior levels when analysts don't have an extensive track record to be judged on.

What determines quality thinking or sound process, independent of the investment outcome? How do we gauge the quality of one analyst's thinking compared to that of another, given differing industry coverage? Ultimately, it comes down to demonstrating an understanding of a business and its risks, and this book will provide a concrete framework for doing so.

The content in the coming pages will apply across asset classes that invest in corporate securities. The goal is to fill in the gaps that a finance degree or related education leaves missing, which typically get addressed on the first one to three years on the job.

WHAT'S MISSING FROM THE STANDARD FINANCE EDUCATION?

There is plenty of educational material around valuation. So much of an investments course or CFA program is centered around projecting cash flows and discounting them at an appropriate rate, and this is important. But being an analyst involves far more judgment than merely knowing how to discount cash flows.

Tools like DCF are useful to illustrate and describe a thesis that one has acquired through the diligence and research process—but that process is itself a separate activity. Current education lacks a structured approach for how to conduct diligence (i.e., what questions to ask, how to know when you've researched enough, etc.), indirectly outsourcing it to the investment banks and related work experiences.

Wouldn't it be useful for you to have access to the pattern-recognition insights such experiences teach while minimizing any unnecessary pains of "touching the hot stove" yourself? This is not to say what I'm offering is a perfect substitute for practical experience. Rather, the frameworks here will be a complement for accelerating the real-world learning process, which can ultimately contribute to quicker promotions and better investment outcomes.

Back to the context of discounted cash flows and valuation, where do the qualitative insights of due diligence fit in? Let's consider the features of typical cash flow mode: projections, growth rates, and discount rates.

What happens when you perform a DCF valuation?

1. You map out your future cash flows on a timeline.
2. You put in an expectation for growth (both during the investment period and in perpetuity).
3. You choose a discount rate for discounting the cash flows.

When you project your cash flows, how do you evaluate the risk and reasonableness of assumptions like "a sales growth of 4%," "a gross profit margin expansion of 250bps," or "$20m in fixed cost savings"?

Further, is the business under analysis the type that can be growing at +10% one year and then -15% the next? Or is it more of a solid +2–3% grower (or negative 2–3% melting ice cube)? Maybe there is a catalyst that provides an immediate step up in revenue (new product, favorable regulation, R&D, etc.) with a flat trajectory thereafter. Similarly, are costs likely to fluctuate or remain steady? What is likely to drive these trajectories?

If you're being thorough, you'll be doing this analysis in not only a base case but also a downside case, thereby "sensitizing" the model and providing a fuller narrative.

But again, how do we ultimately make the judgments on what these growth rates and margin assumptions should be and on how much they should vary?

Whatever your company's situation might be, there's nothing in the spreadsheet model that tells you how to incorporate these assumptions; these are all ideas that *you* bring to the analysis, presumably through questions you've thought about and research you've done.

The quantitative inputs are chosen through the intuition that a *qualitative* analysis of a company generates. Stated alternatively, the conclusions of a qualitative analysis should inevitably appear in the numbers. The numbers are like the tip of the iceberg, and the qualitative components are what drive this visible tip from underneath.

For those who really like analogies and want more than an iceberg... consider a fruit tree. The fruits represent the "numbers" or the actual cash. To correctly project the future status of the fruit harvest, we need to understand whether the tree is getting hydrated and appropriately nourished. What is the quality of the soil? What are the macro elements (e.g., weather patterns) that can impact the growth of this tree? Are weeds being trimmed? Are there any other trees nearby?

By analogy, this is the kind of thinking this handbook will encourage you to use, through an easy-to-use structure that is centered around **spectrums**. Before we discuss the tool of spectrums, allow me to offer more context and a few caveats for the ideas found within the coming pages.

SETTING EXPECTATIONS

Depending on how you slice it, there are over 100 industries, with hundreds, if not thousands, of firms within each. There is simply no way that this book can contain the specific piece of information for the particular company you are analyzing at the moment.

This book won't provide you with the answers directly, but it will provide you the framework to ask the right questions so you can get to your answers.

This book will give you a reliable system to stimulate the process of discovery so you can proactively find that information yourself, rather than being left inadequately prepared and randomly researching or having your portfolio manager direct your efforts.

Consider a few highly relevant on-the-job examples where being able to ask the right questions is crucial:

- You go to a roadshow or lender presentation, and the company hands you a presentation deck that has been surgically crafted by investment bankers to frame the company's story as a good one. Or maybe you're looking at a more innocuous data source such as a 10-K or S-1 filed with the SEC. Either way, you are bombarded with all sorts of information, which may take hours to digest, all while your boss is expecting you to quickly form an objective view.

- You have a unique opportunity to perform diligence and gain critical information about the investment at hand. Perhaps you want to ask a question on a public earnings call for the first time, but don't want to appear foolish (yes, there are dumb questions, when publicly expressed).

- You feel well armed with your thesis when going to pitch it to the investment committee. But then someone asks you a question that you hadn't considered and don't know the answer to. Even worse, others may follow up, poking and prodding to expose your blind spot further.

If you've already experienced these pains, then I believe you'll intuitively see the value in surveying through this book. If you're brand new to investing or exploring a career as an investment professional, ask yourself whether you want to experience these mistakes yourself or learn some lessons from those who have already been there.

As with touching a hot stove, one way to gain knowledge is by experiencing the pain and failures directly, noticing patterns of what works and what doesn't over time. In investment management, you see what kinds of questions your portfolio managers ask, you listen to what gets discussed on quarterly company earnings calls, you discuss the merits of various deals with colleagues... and eventually such experience reduces the frequency of you being surprised by company news and events. In other words, you develop a framework that empowers you to quickly filter and process any piece of company information while contextualizing it into an intelligible investment thesis.

My goal here is to offer you a guide with mental models that, if taken seriously, can help you eliminate 95% of the growing pains in the initial phase of learning.

I believe this book will help you streamline the narrative behind your investment pitches so you can distill the essentials.

This handbook will help you thoughtfully survey through the essential features of a business, so you don't get stumped while speaking at the investment committee. And, broadly speaking, the committee will want to know A) How can I make money on this investment? B) How can I lose money on this investment?[1]

With regard to the former, you have all the ammo you need from the company, investment bank, or private equity sponsor to make your case. But in terms of the latter, it's all on you to fully map out the risks.

Finally, let's remember that investing is ultimately an exercise of making predictions about the future, while bundling these predictions into an organized narrative.

Any sort of prediction entails a direction, degree, dispersion, and dependency.

Direction: The element (revenues, costs, etc.) will either move up or down.

Degree: The element will move by a lot or by a little.

Dispersion: Your estimate of the element will either have a narrow or a wide range of realistic possibilities.

Dependency: Each element is dependent upon or caused by something else.

---

[1] Of course, these questions are also applicable if you are a solo investor.

As an example, this could look like: "I expect revenues (*element*) to go up (*direction*) by 20% (*degree*) based on the company landing this key contract (*dependency*). However, the company has seen delays in the timing of its orders, so it's reasonably likely that this contract doesn't close until next year—if that happens, revenue would be down 5% (*dispersion*), all else being equal."

I'm not going to be explicitly mentioning this framework in the rest of the book, but I recommend it as a starting point for framing your "story" about the investment, as you apply the various spectrum tools that we'll use.

META
FRAMEWORKS

A

INTRO TO SPECTRUM THINKING

Whether we realize it or not, we are constantly evaluating problems and issues by deciding where each of their components lies on a spectrum.

This is apparent when we use explicitly comparative phrases like "too much" or "not enough," as those imply optimal levels that should function as reference points for our judgments. In other words, the "best" or correct amount of something exists between a spectrum of 0% and 100%, and we observe that the current value of what we're looking at is either above or below this ideal threshold.

The context of spectrums is also applicable when we make normative judgments, labeling things as either "good" or "bad." While these classifications may seem like they stand on their own ("This is good." "That is bad."), the intelligent thinker will always ask: "Good or bad... *compared to what*?" This engages the mind to contemplate alternatives and rank-order them along a spectrum.

Let's drill this in first with some non-business examples. When thinking about governmental systems, we often see the tug-of-war between individual freedom and centralized control. Assuming we do consider these to be opposing forces, we can contemplate them in the context of a spectrum. On one end, where you have complete, unconstrained individual freedom, we place the outcome of Anarchy. On the other end, where government holds total control at the expense of personal freedom, we put Totalitarianism. Back along the freedom portion, but more toward the middle relative to Anarchy, we consider Libertarian points of view. And along the governmental control portion, we place extremely centralized forms of Socialism to the inside of Totalitarianism.

A Hypothetical Spectrum for Political Systems

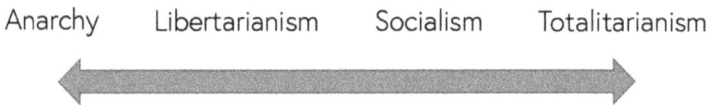

Anarchy   Libertarianism   Socialism   Totalitarianism

$\longleftrightarrow$

Spectrum thinking can be used to navigate through the most dangerous and divisive conversations. Don't believe me? Let's see how this tool can help us calmly sift through the most controversial and emotionally jarring of topics.

Consider the opinions surrounding something like abortion. Regardless of one's political leaning, the discussion generally requires some assessment of when human "rights" begin. What would the spectrum be for this? On one end, you could place Conception.

On the other end you could put Birth.[2] Then you can debate where the optimal sweet spot for the origin of "human rights" lies along this spectrum. Framed in this manner, you can encourage a more productive dialogue compared to the more unhelpful, shouting alternatives. Conversational participants can get to a more amiable point of "agree to disagree," where each can understand the other's opinions with greater specificity, ideally bypassing any amygdalic ad hominems or straw men.

I'll give another political example, which is especially pertinent at the time of this chapter's initial draft: addressing COVID-19 compared to mitigating economic fallout. What's the spectrum? Visually set upper and lower bounds. On one end of the spectrum you can envision business as usual, with no regard for the pandemic, to keep the economy chugging along, at the expense of overwhelming hospitals and getting more deaths. On the other end of the spectrum you could see indefinite shutdown, destroying GDP but saving more lives from the virus, while converting the basic structures of human interaction to virtual.[3]

I give political examples here because they are generally abstract, complex, and bias-inducing in nature, and spectrum thinking can

---

[2] I suppose you could theoretically place the other end at some point after birth, but that would exceed the traditional scope of the debate, as it would then become about human rights in general.

[3] I framed this spectrum before the various country lockdowns happened. Then governments showed signs of moderation as they seriously weighed the impact to the economy. This is reliably what seems to happen, by the way: People will initially think in one dimension (e.g., "Prevent deaths no matter what!") until they start experiencing the negative externalities of such end-of-spectrum reactions and then moderate accordingly.

help debias and concretize the discussion. You can use spectrums for anything, however, whether it be ingredient trade-offs in cooking, ranges of kinesthetic motion in athletics, or attitudes and emotions in relationships.

You might be wondering... "How does all of this apply to investing? This is a business book, after all!"

For the sake of an example more in the ballpark of daily portfolio decision-making, think about the familiar paradigm that conceptualizes investor behavior along a spectrum of fear vs. greed, the bounds between which market sentiments fluctuate. Some of your best trade ideas have likely priced in an assumption of where sentiment for a particular security lies between these two states. Identifying the current sweet spot on the fear vs. greed spectrum is a necessary condition to capitalize on the old investing adage of "Buy when everyone is selling and sell when everyone is buying." In plain English, you would ask: "Where does the market's current sentiment lie between the extremes of paralyzing, panicking fear and blindly insatiable greed?"

Intuitively you may already see the immense value of applying spectrum thinking. Testing the upper and lower bounds of an idea, not unlike turning the volume knob of a guitar amplifier from 0 to 10 and then back to somewhere in the middle, will solidify your understanding of an idea's context, possibilities, and relative positioning.[4]

---

[4] Relative value frameworks are an investor's bread and butter, and the conscious application of spectrum analysis to individual aspects of a company's business model will take your analysis a crucial leap further, giving you a consistent tool to quickly make informed value judgments.

Whether you have precise conviction on where the optimal point along a given spectrum is, the framing of conversation around the relative positioning of alternatives along that spectrum will demonstrate tremendous competence.

More importantly, you'll gain the confidence that you've minimized your cognitive blind spots and explored all the most relevant aspects of an investment thesis.

Before we jump into the practical tools (the spectrums), it's worthwhile to establish some context on business models, which will productively frame the rest of our analysis.

B

PRODUCT VS. SERVICE
BUSINESS MODEL FRAMEWORKS

"What does this company do?"

You cannot understand the risk of an investment if you do not understand the business model of the company. The two go hand in hand.

To comprehend an investment's overall risk at a meaningful level, we need to understand the underlying business model at a comparatively meaningful level, asking the most useful, exploratory questions possible. We'll know we've achieved a sufficient grasp if we are able to explain the entire business model in a way that a fifth grader would understand.[5]

The first step to assimilating the business model of a particular company is to ask yourself, "*What problem(s) is this company trying to solve?*"

---

[5] This often-used analogy is a high-level characterization. Granularly speaking, I would emphasize a focus on speaking in visual terms, painting a tangible picture of what's happening, showcasing the relationships of the relevant counterparties through illustrative stories.

If you ever find yourself getting lost in the thick of the weeds scrambling through pages and pages of information, bring your awareness back to this clarifying thought. It will serve as the anchor for all the further company insights that you will gain.

In considering the problem being solved, we need to determine whether the company is offering a product, service, or both, recognizing whether there are multiple products and/or services, which may each solve distinct problems.

Sometimes this is straightforward, especially if it's a company that you know well. You may say, for example, that a restaurant solves the problem of hunger, offering its customers prepared food as a solution. We can even take it a step further and say that, in addition to food, the restaurant offers a leisure experience through its execution of service and atmosphere, in a way that addresses the problem of boredom.[6]

Arguably the best starting point in finding out what a company does is to go to the "Business" section on their 10-K, if they are publically traded, or through the memorandum posted on the company's deal site.[7] It's a healthy exercise to analyze the description and determine whether it will have to be broken down further for comprehension.

Let's look first at the description statement of a prominent and well-followed company such as Apple:

---

[6] While these kinds of distinctions may seem esoteric, they often lead to new insights around a company's differentiation.

[7] Of course, there are other alternatives—you could visit the company's website, pull the ticker up on your Bloomberg terminal, phone a friend...

"The Company designs, manufactures and markets smartphones, personal computers, tablets, wearables and accessories, and sells a variety of related services."[8]

This statement is clear enough, especially compared to upcoming examples, other than some ambiguity at the end of the sentence ("a variety of related services"), which gets clarified a couple of paragraphs further into the 10-K.

Here is one way we can retranslate the basic idea of this business: Apple provides stylish hardware (smartphones, laptops, wearables) that solves the problem of customers wanting to interact with the internet, utilize various apps, and manage documents in a user-friendly fashion.

This example is easy to comprehend not only because it's a company many know and love but also because its description is stated plainly.

But what about a business that's more complex and obscure? Take, for example, some other real-world 10-K descriptions, where a company under consideration is described as:

- "a leading provider of merchant acquiring and commercial payments solutions";

- "a global provider of infrastructure solutions for communication and entertainment networks";

- "a global technology company providing commerce solutions that power billions of transactions";

---

[8] Apple's FY2019 10-K.

- "a leading nationwide provider of end-to-end healthcare technology management and service solutions to the United States healthcare industry";

- "a tech-enabled provider of comprehensive retirement and investment solutions."

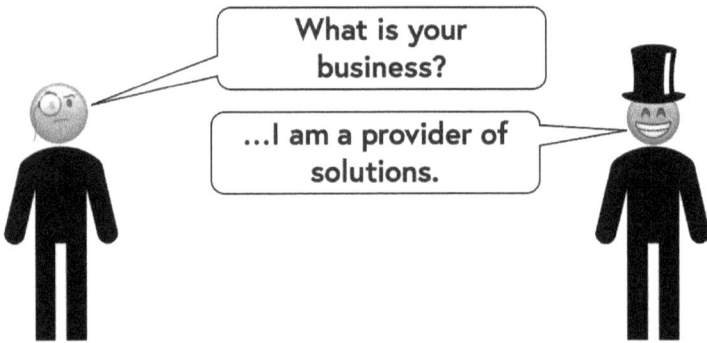

Do we know what any of these sentences *actually* mean? If this was the only information you had, would you be able to visualize a scene in your mind representing what each of these companies does? Could you explain their businesses coherently to a fifth grader? Probably not.

We'll need to dig further to understand the businesses, and the spectrums provide an organized and systematic fashion for acquiring that understanding. The spectrums give you tools of questioning to look behind the layers of company jargon.

Notice that each company is described as a "provider" of some kind of "solution,"[9] but this information is insufficient on its own. Even if we knew what the solution (i.e., product/service) being offered was, a business model involves more than just a product or service. Let's use the following image for inspiration.

An Illustration of Every Business

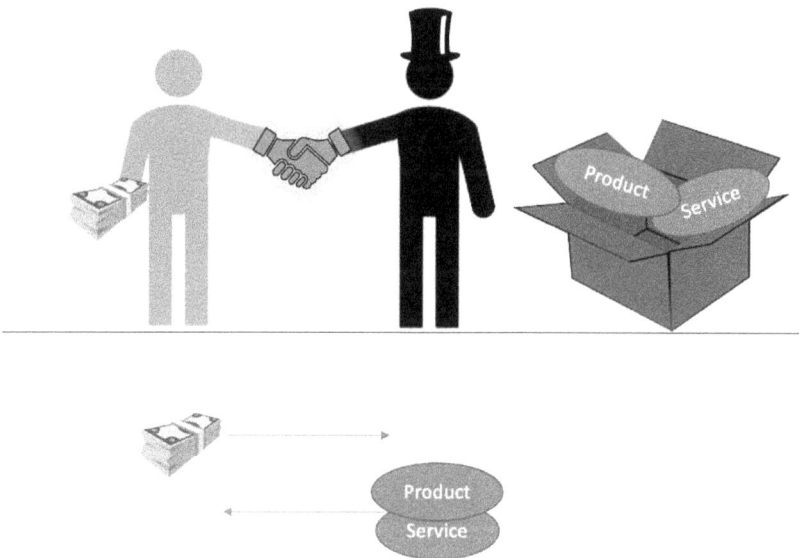

This picture represents the fundamental unit of what makes a business: a transaction between a buyer and a seller, where one party exchanges money for a product or service.

---

[9] Given the importance of our anchor question ("What problems does your company solve?"), does it surprise you that companies love to use this word? Rather than writing "product or service" ad nauseum, I will use this word as well.

We will continue our analysis on companies' products and services (i.e., "solutions"), in addition to exploring the characteristics of the customers and suppliers, along with the nature of the "handshake" or revenue stream.

Further, using the **right** side of the image as reference, we will be dealing with the spectrums of a product or service offering, in terms of its characteristics, production, and distribution.

On the **left** side we see a customer, which will represent our focus on the nature and desires of those who purchase the product or service.

And in the **middle**, where the "handshake" is, we will apply spectrums to the structural and contractual nature of the agreement to trade goods and services for money.

With the theoretical framework set, let's analyze the various spectrums in business risk.

A QUICK NOTE ON THE ORDERING OF SPECTRUMS

There are many ways in which one could organize and order the spectrums of risk, and each decision would be arbitrary. I've grouped these tools into categories that I think can be useful, but you can certainly reclassify them in your mind with no sacrifice in analysis.

Determining which feature spectrum is most important will depend upon the specific investment situation at a given time. Therefore, it's worth clarifying that the spectrums outlined in earlier parts of this book are not necessarily more or less important than those handled later.

Some spectrums will offer more insight than others, and each will provide a different way to frame the considered business whether you are analyzing it by yourself or discussing it with others. Furthermore, an individual concept may not be mind-blowing on its own, but the sum of all the lenses will provide you with a comprehensive high-level understanding and a peace of mind in that you've touched on most, if not all, blind spots. Translation: You will feel and sound like you know what you're talking about.

Finally, note that some spectrums will have a good feature on one end and a bad feature on the other end. Others will have a continuum where one part of the spectrum isn't necessarily worse than the other but instead offers a different set of risks. Either way, if a company's business model is "bad" in light of one spectrum, it may be "good" when viewed through the lens of another. It is ultimately up to you, the analyst, to weigh and aggregate the various insights that arise from each spectrum, as you arrive at your overall assessment of a business's risk.

SPECTRUMS

PRODUCTS AND SERVICES

1

VALUE-ADD SPECTRUM:

PHILOSOPHY OF THE VALUE CHAIN

One of the first steps in understanding a business model and its related risks is to classify its role along a value chain. Doing so will provide a meta starting point that will allow us to interpret all the other spectrums. Further, the goal of this section is to offer a standardized approach that you can apply to any kind of business model.

To begin, with your considered business in mind, attempt to visualize the entire cause and effect chain of its product or service, starting from the natural resources and raw materials needed to produce it, through the intermediary nodes of distribution, all the way to the end customer making a purchase.

Repeat this exercise in the reverse direction in order to adequately picture the flow of money, which starts from the end customer's pocket and flows through the intermediaries all the way down to the beginning of the supply chain.[10]

---

[10] Some value chains have a flow of money and goods that is multi-directional, and perhaps not linear. An example is the travel GDS industry, which receives cash

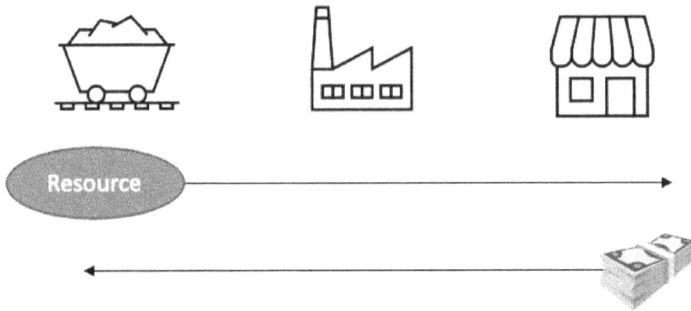

This may sound simple enough, but you'd be surprised how often doing this exercise exposes glaring knowledge gaps in what otherwise felt like a solid grasp of a business.

One manner in thinking about this topic is to divide the types of value chains based on whether there is a product or service being sold to the end user.

TANGIBLE GOODS

For businesses that deal with products or tangible goods, the company will generally be one of the following: a manufacturer, intermediary distributor, or a direct seller (e.g., retailer or sales rep) to the end user.

---

from both the airlines and hotels and the business travelers it serves, with each party functioning both as a supplier and customer, in different respects.

Consider something we all love: food. On the left side of value chain spectrum, you have agricultural businesses that harvest grains, vegetables, and livestock, functioning as primary manufacturers. These harvested raw materials might then go to a food products manufacturer, who combines them into a frozen meal, a cereal, or some other culinary item, thereby functioning as a secondary manufacturer. If this company doesn't do it themselves, it might then send its product to a packager who finalizes the good to be ready for sale. Then, after some stops at warehouses and other transportation hubs, the good gets moved to a grocery store, where an individual consumer can grab it off the shelf, representing the rightmost part of the spectrum. And let's not forget that between each node lie various logistics providers (distributors operating planes, trains, and automobiles).

Alternatively, in this example of food, you can think about some of the agricultural products going directly to retail, in the form of being served at a restaurant or laid out in the fresh produce segment of your local farmers market, skipping some of those intermediate nodes.

Working backward, visualize at checkout the cash (or credit card) payment being transferred from the customer's wallet to the store, which keeps a portion of the funds and passes the rest on to distributors, food product manufacturers, and so on.

Another example of a tangible good's value chain would be a typical consumer gadget. At the primary node on the chain, you would have a mining company procuring raw metals from the ground. These metals then get refined through an industrial manufacturing process, which requires energy (which depends upon burning natural resources attained from other drilling or mining activities). Perhaps plastics and semiconductor manufacturers are added into the mix, contributing individual components. Then, you might have a specialty chemical company imparting various features onto the raw materials such as heat-resistance or color. After the components get combined into a ready-for-sale product at an assembly plant, you can move it into distribution channels (e.g., warehouses), and sell it through retail or direct to consumer (e.g., online).

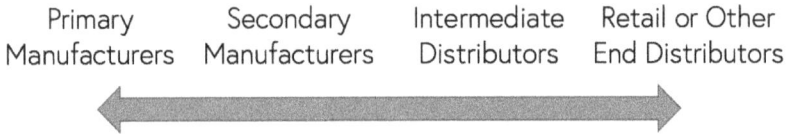

Primary Manufacturers	Secondary Manufacturers	Intermediate Distributors	Retail or Other End Distributors

$\longleftrightarrow$

SERVICES

Services companies will either be classified on a node somewhere along these product value chains, as is the case with distributors[11] (who provide services that facilitate the movement of a product), or they will be part of a separate chain that deals primarily with services being sold to end users.

A simple example of the latter kind would be your local barber or salon. You pay them cash to perform *some action*—in this case,

---

[11] We can also consider leasing business models a service tied to a product chain, as the lease offers you the service of accessing the use of a product for a preset period of time as opposed to owning it outright.

cutting your hair. The service provider may need to purchase products, such as a shaver or scissors, in order to perform their action. But ultimately the raw material of a service company (and the primary node of the service value chain) is its human capital, the real people performing the action being sold.

Compared to a tangible good that you can actually hold in your hand, what exactly is a consumer paying for when they order a service?

The consumer is purchasing access to some combination of expertise, efficiency, or entertainment. And in some sense, the consumer is purchasing a form of labor, not unlike how any company "purchases" labor when it hires its employees.

In light of this characterization, you wouldn't be wrong in viewing all service companies as outsource plays carrying out certain tasks on the customer's behalf.

The salon cuts Jessica's hair so that she doesn't have to. The construction company builds the house so that Joe avoids a life-sized Jenga incident. The doctor performs the surgery so the patient doesn't have to...

MEDIA AND OTHER EXPERIENCES

How can we apply the value chain framework to businesses that sell media or enable access to a platform? Should we use the product or service framework?

Well, it's more of an academic distinction than something with practical consequence, as you can look at it both ways.

Take the example of a live entertainment event, such as a music concert, sports game, or theater performance. From a product paradigm, you could say that the venue and event organizer are providing you with an *intangible* product or experience, which you consume. The real-time experience depletes as the show proceeds, yet the event "product" also leaves you with some residual good or piece of knowledge that gets stored in your memory. So, in some respects, it's a product that gets consumed immediately, and in other respects it's a product you hold onto forever.

Through a service paradigm, you could think about the live event experience as a service being delivered by the artists or athletes to the spectators. The act of service is completed when the event ends. Perhaps this framework doesn't feel as intellectually satisfying, but notice how we use analogous language in our culture for some live events, such as a church "service."

What about paying to watch movies? Are you buying a movie "product"? Paying for a broadcasting "service"? Purchasing "rights" (intangible goods) to receive visual and aural sensory stimulation?

You can conduct this thought experiment ad nauseam, but ultimately the point is to categorize these media businesses within the context of having raw materials (the performers and the venue), a manufacturing process (directing, editing, and overall production), and a distribution channel to reach the end user.

For simplicity, I would suggest classifying this category of businesses, which also includes video games, leisure activities, and other solutions, as involving businesses that sell you the product of a particular *experience*.

PLATFORMS

When considering the business model of a social media platform—or really that of any website—it's now commonly understood that revenue comes from advertisers rather than users. Users often don't pay for access to a particular website or product of experience. Instead, advertisers are the customers, and the platform supplies them with the product of consumer attention (views, impressions, etc.), which you and I supply.

An alternative conceptualization is to suggest that platforms sell the service of distribution, in the sense of providing advertisers a virtual shelf-space to promote their products. This would mean the website is implicitly functioning like a retailer or an entertainment venue, in which a third-party vendor sets up a promotional stand. You don't go to the store or venue with the intention of stopping by a pop-up booth, but if the stand catches your eye while you're in there, you might check it out. The same holds true for how you handle that ad sitting on the side of a web page.

How do websites procure the raw materials of human attention? As already noted, in traditional businesses, the supply of human capital or labor is acquired through cash. In other words, businesses pay their employees to give their attention. But in the case of platforms, the supply of attention is acquired through the currency of interesting "content," or more specifically, through the currency of dopamine.[12]

---

[12] On a neurological level, we might say that consumers exchange money primarily for hits of dopamine, particularly when it comes to discretionary spending. If we

Like removing gold from rocks, we can say that content providers extract the intangible natural resource of human attention from people, except through a "mining" process that is more dynamic and ever-changing. What is most successful at capturing and extracting attention now will look like something else in the future.

TECHNOLOGY

Is technology a product or a service? If you reference the company descriptions in the prior chapter, you'll know that the correct answer is... neither—it's a solution! (Just kidding.)

To actually answer this, we need to slice technology up into subsectors. There are many ways to do this, but for our purposes here, let's divide it into two: hardware vs. software.

Hardware business models neatly fit into the product value chain framework. We can refer back to our earlier example of a consumer gadget or think about a similar value chain for equipment that is sold to enterprises. Furthermore, hardware businesses often involve not only an up-front product sale but also a maintenance service that gets "attached" to the product.

Sometimes a business might sell access to hardware. The main model that comes to my mind is that of a cloud provider who sells storage, space, or connectivity on a monthly recurring fee basis. At

---

agree that's a fair depiction, we can treat the mediums of cash and dopamine as ultimately fungible.

this point the business model starts to blend in with that of other telecommunications or commodity providers.

Software is where it gets more esoteric again, as its characterization echoes with the kinds of distinctions we discussed around media and content—namely, purchasing a product of experience versus a service of access.

The software industry operates under both frameworks. A firm selling a perpetual license for a piece of software might recognize that as a product sale. Within tech job titles, there is also the clear moniker of *product* management. Yet, solutions like software-as-a-service (SaaS) offerings operate—as the names would suggest—through subscription-based *service* revenue models.

Either way, the "manufacturing" process of software involves some organization of software engineers who craft the code and design the user interface that overlays it. Distribution options vary. In the past, you may have picked up a physical copy of a CD at an electronics retailer. Now, you can get the software delivered through a web app on the cloud.

Those with an economics background might recall a third way we can look at "technology" that spans beyond software, hardware, and general computing. In the Cobb-Douglas function,[13] technology is linked to the factor of productivity. As you increase productivity, you improve the output that your labor and capital can produce. So, under this formulation, a technology provider is selling

---

[13] The Cobb-Douglas function is: $Y = AK^\alpha L^{1-\alpha}$, which effectively states that total production (Y) equals the interaction of capital (K) and labor (L), multiplied by the coefficient of productivity (A).

the intangible force of productivity, at least when making an enterprise sale.

FINANCIAL SERVICES

As the name would suggest, firms in the financial sector are typically offering a *service* in facilitating the movement of money. Yet here we also see firms, such as asset managers, talking about the creation and distribution of *products*, with ETFs, mutual funds, and other securities being prime examples.

When thinking about the value chain for financial firms, a unique feature stands out. Money is not only a form of payment for the good or service being distributed but is also the raw material or is itself the solution provided to the buyer.

In that case, what exactly is the client paying for? Why pay money in order to receive money?

The money being used as the raw material—this can be AUM or bank deposits, for example—is then taken through a "manufacturing" process and "invested." If all goes according the plan, the money is multiplied and returned to the money supplier (who also functions as the client), less a fee charged for this service of multiplication. Again, the cash leaves the client, goes through the production process of investing, and then comes back to the client.

The production process of investing almost always involves some contractual agreement where one party sells the intangible "product" of a promise to send cash at some point in the future.[14] While there is eventually a two-sided movement of cash, there is immediately an asymmetrical exchange of time and risk. One party gets clear certainty of getting money now, whereas the other party undertakes more uncertainty in agreeing to receive the money in the future, adding an up-charge to offset this lopsidedness.

Let's better illustrate this concept in the reverse scenario, where the client wants to *receive* money up front, and pay for this privilege later. The most familiar case is when someone receives a loan from the bank.

Bob wants $100,000 to pay for part of a house, so he goes to the bank, presumably because he doesn't have the $100k himself. His problem is that he wants cash *now*. The solution is that he will acquire this cash today through the promise of paying the bank cash *later*. In some sense, Bob sells to the bank the intangible product of a promise.

How does this fit into the "production process of investing"? When Bob borrows money, the bank is effectively investing in him, with the hope of being paid back more in the future, in the form of interest. Furthermore, you could also consider this situation one where Bob functions as a de facto asset manager on behalf of the bank, taking $100k in AUM and providing a return. Comparing a private borrower to an asset manager may seem strange, but understanding this analogy will help clear up more complicated financial business models.

---

[14] This is true for virtually any investment. Stocks, bonds, options, and other derivatives are all merely contractual agreements to move money among parties at some contingent point in the future.

We can swap out Bob with a firm requiring cash in order to expand its operations, and the effect remains the same. The business gets cash *now* by selling the promise of paying back its investors in the future. This business goes through an "investing" process of its own, where it multiplies the money through the engine of its operations, which ultimately hinge upon raw end consumer demand for a product or service. Through this conceptualization we can now say that all businesses not only sell their typical products or services to potential consumers but also sell the promises of cash multiplication to potential investors, with the value of the promises being subject to various idiosyncratic and macroeconomic factors.

Each promise to receive cash now and pay more cash later can be represented as a node in the flow of money. Arranging all the nodes in sequence, we can present an illustrative investing value chain.

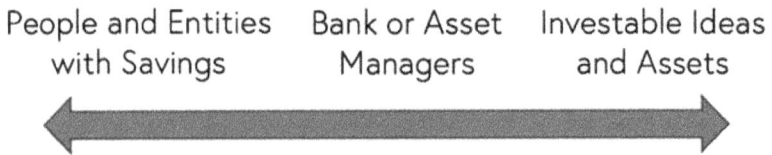

People and Entities   Bank or Asset   Investable Ideas
with Savings   Managers   and Assets

⟵―――――――――――――――――――――――⟶

On the far left, we might start with retained earnings or consumer savings, which function as the initial supply of raw materials. These funds might then get moved to a bank or asset manager to be taken through the "production" process of investing. The production process requires an investment idea (on the right side), which most commonly appears as a company or an individual requiring capital for the purposes of funding revenue-generating operations or acquiring an asset. Once the money is moved into the hands of such a party, it gets deployed into the "engine" that multiplies it. This multiplication ultimately happens by way of a company purchasing labor, capital, or technology, which subsequently allows the company to raise its prices or sell more volumes to end customers, increasing total revenues. Greater total revenues, all else being equal, will lead to more cash flow, which eventually gets funneled back down to the investors along the money supply chain, with each party taking its respective cut.

In addition to operating companies buying revenue-generating assets, other scenarios of money multiplication exist as final nodes. One such example is a sovereign government printing money (multiplying money in a very literal sense) and either sending it back to bondholders, fulfilling its "promise," or deploying the money into the broader economy, by giving it directly to companies or individuals.

Another example of a rightmost node is an M&A or LBO transaction whereby the acquirer purchases the target and pays off the existing debtholders and stockholders. In other words, the competitor or private equity firm purchasing the operating company sends cash to the existing investors of that company. This action serves as the cash-multiplying engine that fulfills the promises to the investors.

Now, I used the term "rightmost" for ease of understanding, but when it comes to the flow of money (the core business of financial firms) and a fully functioning economy, the value "chain" ends up being circular, or a network of interconnecting lines that branch across multiple categories and industry verticals. In other words, money—and the financial firms that move it around—is involved in every kind of business, so this product doesn't have a clear origin and end point, unlike other products, which clearly originate in a factory and are ultimately consumed.[15]

Hopefully, all these illustrations are sufficient in giving you a clear picture for constructing a value chain for any financial firm that bases its business model on generating investment returns.

For other financial services firms, such as payment processors, brokers, or alternative currency providers, the concepts remain relatively the same. Just consider those models as ones where the "product" of money moves through a distribution network, where each distributor takes a cut for providing their service of product movement.

---

[15] At the risk of beating a dead horse, bring your attention to that "rightmost" value chain node of an operating company deploying capital in order to generate more revenues. The new revenues come from consumers, who received their cash from, say, their employers, who received their cash from the sale of products or services to other consumers, who received their cash from employers or investments... And so it goes, on and on. Furthermore, the cash at any point can be used, in part, as raw material that goes into an investment production process elsewhere, creating a web of branches within our circular value chains.

CONCLUDING THOUGHTS

While the examples explored in this chapter are by no means exhaustive, they should provide you with enough frameworks to deal with most business models. These are starting points that will help you explain a business in very simple terms. Furthermore, we can infer some generalized insights depending on whether the company is located toward the beginning of the value chain (raw materials, manufacturing), the middle (distribution), or the end (final point-of-sale).

2

DISCRETIONALITY (NEED-TO-EXIST)

One of the most popular questions an investment analyst or portfolio manager asks is: "Does this business need to exist?" Is it highly discretionary or critically essential?

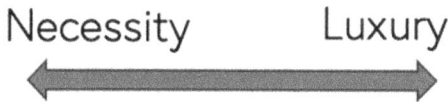

Necessity   Luxury

⟵————————————————⟶

This implied spectrum of discretionality is fairly self-explanatory. Intuitively, we know that certain products or services are more objectively needed compared to others, whose demand is based more on subjective desires and consumer preferences.

Phrased alternatively, if products that "need" to exist disappeared overnight, there would be some structural damage and actual loss, compared to the absence of discretionary products, which may only result in temporarily sad customers who will ultimately move their attention elsewhere.

Of course, if you want get overly philosophical, you could have the debate of whether anything actually "needs" to exist, but please humor me in considering this topic through the lens of practicality and relative value. And in case it needs to be said, just because a company's particular product or service may need to exist, it doesn't mean *that* specific company needs to exist.

Let's consider a few categories[16] of businesses whose solutions are located toward the "need-to-exist" camp:

- *Infrastructure and energy-related* industries, which serve as the structural backbone for society. Power generators, utilities, oil and gas companies, construction, telecommunications, scaled transportation and logistics providers, and the various service providers associated with these (some being more essential than others).

- *Raw materials and industrial* industries, which provide the critical early ingredients for other manufacturing processes. Metals and mining operations, agriculture, textiles, many chemical producers, industrial components and equipment manufacturers, and so on.

- *Regulatory-driven* industries, or those that will always have a floor of demand because the government mandates that the products or services of the industry exist. Various insurance providers (car, health, homeowner's, workers' comp, etc.), auditors, law firms, companies that have the government as

---

[16] There will be some overlap here (e.g., energy is, in many ways, a raw material).

their primary or sole customer (including aspects of Defense), and so on.

- *Other critical financial services*, which provide the lubrication for a smooth-functioning economy. Banks, mortgage originators, payment processors, certain asset managers, credit card companies, and so on.

- *Well-being essentials*, including various healthcare providers (hospitals, certain pharmaceuticals and medical equipment providers) and the necessity of broad categories such as food or clothing (though in their specific applications, these latter two are almost always highly discretionary, as will be discussed below), or even media.

To generalize from this list, we can say that if these companies ceased to exist it would result in any of the following: a B2B customer's supply chain disruption,[17] an end consumer experiencing loss at a primary Maslow level, or an angry government.

On the discretionary camp, we lump in the "nice-to-have" categories, such as most consumer products, hotels, and travel and leisure, in addition to outsourcing players (and many technology companies can be categorized as such), which are discussed in the section for the value chain spectrum.

---

[17] In this vein, many companies will try to signal a "need-to-exist" quality by using terms like "mission-critical." Sometimes this is valid, but always question such designations.

Food products and clothing are interesting cases, because the industries in aggregate need to exist, but virtually any specific product within the industry doesn't need to exist. In other words, both the product categories and the brands within each category are immensely fragmented and readily substitutable, even though the existence of the concept (food or clothing) itself is very critical and not disposable.

You might even make an interesting case for a similar necessity of media, sports, entertainment... bundled into the all-encompassing category of "art" or "stories." Is any specific event or production necessary? No. But what would happen to the stability of society if there were no more movies, games, or online content? Maybe the currently massive database of historical content is sufficient to address this distinctly human need, but we'll leave that thought experiment to be solved for the future.

This focus on fragmentation brings us to an important correlation found within this spectrum. The more discretionary a business is, the more heavily it will rely on branding to drive sales. Compare the branding needs of an independent power producer bidding into the electricity markets to those of a cosmetics company persuading consumers to adopt its particular strand of beauty. Not only can you consider directionality a risk to revenues, but also you can keep in mind the amount of sales and marketing spending that is necessary to keep the business flat.

Up until now, this spectrum of discretionality has been viewed through the purview of product categories and industries. But we can also stratify the discretionality within a given sector. This is done simply when we think about tiering of products (good vs. better vs.

best; premium vs. low-cost; luxury vs. mass-produced, etc.), in addition to substitutability. For example, I can upgrade my basic peanut butter to organic peanut butter. Or I can make a further discretional upgrade by substituting it for some specialty artisan nut butter.

The same motifs regarding importance of branding and subjective preference come into full force when looking at items priced at the high end, even for industries that are more essential. A great example of this is what happened in the mattress industry to the incumbent players such as Serta Simmons, who enjoyed dominant market share leadership and had most of its mattresses priced well over $1,000. Mattresses "need" to exist, but do $1,000+ mattresses need to exist? The industry was then disrupted by the mattress-in-a-box products, which were superior in terms of convenience and price (many at a sub-$200 price tag).

So, in considering the business risk of such a profile, you might say that the company's product category needs to exist but that its relative positioning within the category is highly discretionary. Hence such a business model still has some elements of discretionary risk.[18]

We've discussed some examples on each end of the discretionality / need-to-exist spectrum. What could go in the middle? That's ultimately for you to determine on a case-by-case basis, but this could naturally include categories such as automobiles, education, or even homeownership, which all contain material elements of both necessity and discretion.

---

[18] To tease out this distinction, you can contrast the profile to a brand, such as Rolex, which has discretionary positioning within a discretionary product.

3

DIY VS. DIFM

Many business solutions can be plotted along a spectrum of DIY vs. DIFM, where demand for the product or service is related to a consumer preference of solving problems themselves vs. hiring others to solve those problems.

DIY   DIFM

A natural DIY example that may come to mind is your local home improvement store, whose demand largely relies on consumers buying paint, wood, screws, and so on for home renovations.

Another case is an aftermarket auto parts provider, which supplies replacement parts and added accessories for your car. Generally, these businesses will rely on consumer DIY initiatives (though the larger companies have diversified to also have DIFM demand exposure in selling to the professionals who will respond to the "do-it-for-me" requests).

Aside from the cases where the terminology is explicitly used, can we apply this thinking to other industries?

Consider the financial advisory business, particularly private wealth management. On one end of the spectrum, you have retail brokerages, such as E-Trade and Robinhood, where the platform is geared toward a DIY customer who wants to make the asset allocation and stock selection decisions independently. On the other end, which is in the DIFM realm, you have RIAs, IBDs, or big bank wirehouses who will manage your portfolio for you for a fee. Then, when you think of novel, hybrid ideas, such as robo-advisory, you can plot them along the continuum somewhere in between.

Extending the application further, you can apply this filter to food-related businesses. A grocery store would generally fall into the DIY category, as it serves the demand for those who want to purchase food and prepare the meal at home. On the other hand, restaurants would be in the DIFM category given that they prepare the food for you.

You can slide the scale even further toward DIFM when you consider food delivery apps, such as Grubhub, which do the traveling part of acquiring food for you. And then perhaps somewhere in the middle of the spectrum, we can place meal kit services, which have some balance of DIY vs. DIFM elements.[19]

A final point to note is that DIFM solutions are generally more discretionary. However, for certain tasks that require high levels of competency, DIFM may be the only practical option for the consumer to choose.

---

[19] Note that in the food service industry, the paradigm of a "Food Away from Home" (FAFH) mix has generally been used, but conceptually it's still a DIY vs. DIFM decision, albeit with a different label.

4

PERISHABILITY AND THE REPLACEMENT CYCLE

Thinking about the perishability of goods will give you a sense of inventory management and timing of consumer purchasing behavior.

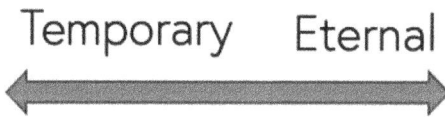

Temporary   Eternal

⟵——————————————⟶

On one end of the spectrum, you have highly perishable (and readily consumable) goods like food products, particularly dairy, fresh produce, and meats. On the other, we could consider long-lived assets with multiple decades of useful life, which include houses or infrastructure-related properties.

Products with a short useful life need to be moved through distribution and turned over faster than those with longer lives. This implies a comparative need for higher sales and promotional activity, in addition to timeliness of logistics. Moreover, perishable products are more likely to have spoilage costs, which occur when the product deteriorates before it is successfully sold. In cases such as these, it becomes critical to determine who bears the risk of a spoiled product. Does a distributor fully front the cost of the product, or do they only pay the OEM once a sale to an end consumer has been made?

Consider the contrast of business activities surrounding a grocery item versus those around a house. On average, a house can remain in inventory for much longer than the food product that is set to expire in a few days. Barring any other situational pressures, the seller of a long-lived asset has more optionality in extending a sale process, whereas the retailer of a perishable item will, practically speaking, be forced to slash prices and get the product off the shelf.

This factor is double-edged, of course, in that buyers of long-lived assets are comparatively less prevalent, given their option to continue utilizing their existing long-lived asset as opposed to having to make a purchase. In other words, a liquidity differential generally exists along this spectrum of perishability, with longer-lived assets being less liquid, of course.

Extending this concept to consumer goods, hardware companies, or products that are in the middle of the two poles of perishability, you'll often hear companies discussing the "replacement cycle." Aptly named, this refers to how often a consumer replaces the product in question with an equivalent or newer version, whether by necessity or choice.

In the food product example, we covered the aspect of necessity that is mandated by nature. Another aspect of necessity is driven by regulation or prevailing industry standards. An interesting example is what happened to credit card manufacturing companies a handful of years ago. Prior to the advent of EMV chip cards, credit card replacement cycles (i.e., those based on that expiry date you see on your card) were three to four years. Then, due to increases in card resiliency, among other factors, the industry standard shifted to three to five years. To use averages, the replacement cycle extended from ~3.5 years to ~4 years. Even though the product quality improved and consumer credit card spending continued to increase, the ultimate revenue impact from this factor alone was -12.5%,[20] which is enough to send a levered company into distress (see CPI Card).

Replacement cycles are often subject to dynamic consumer preferences, rather than fixed constants. If you look at investing in a company like Callaway, the replacement cycle becomes critical. In this case, a golf club replacement cycle might be two to three years. However, given the relatively discretionary nature of the product, you would be wise to consider how this cycle might shift during periods of economic downturn, as consumers delay that purchase. A similar example of discretionary replacement behavior occurs with new automobiles, which would also flex in terms of extended replacement cycles, or outright substitution, in the face of economic hardships.

Technology has an interesting influence on replacement cycles as it imparts both features of necessity and discretion. According to Moore's Law, computing power doubles every two years (today this is more like 2.5 years), thereby creating an eventual need for users to upgrade their equipment.

---

[20] $(1/4) / (1/3.5) - 1.$

A recent enterprise example occurred in the ATM industry, whose products generally have had eight-to-ten-year cycles. Many of these machines run on Windows software, and when Microsoft announced it would be discontinuing support for its older operating systems, ATM operators were effectively forced to upgrade their fleet to run on Windows 10. However, some of the older machines couldn't handle the new software load, so that particular replacement cycle accelerated, given the technological pressure to upgrade, leading to an acceleration of near-term sales.

An example on the consumer side of tech occurred when smartphones were released. As the changes in technology at that time were more leap-like as opposed to gradual, consumers were keeping pace with a ~2-year replacement cycle. Now, existing phones hold their relevance longer by way of having all the core, sexy features (access to apps, camera, etc.) while improvements in new phones have become more incremental in nature (slightly higher megapixels, better resolution, etc.). The perceived need for consumers to upgrade has decreased; hence the replacement cycle has now extended closer to three years. This may change with the next generation of technology, but it's TBD on that.

When considering risks associated with perishability and replacement cycles, the key aspects to focus on are the length and malleability of the cycles. Longer cycles are generally riskier, as they imply a lower margin for error. For example, if your competitor wins the customer for a product with a seven-year cycle, you might not be able to win that customer back until those seven years have elapsed. A longer frequency also implies comparatively fewer product iterations and a slower-moving industry. The positive offset to this is that industries with long replacement cycles often have higher barriers to entry.

With regard to malleability, we have already seen how cycles can change based on extraneous factors. The purpose in considering this risk is to inform the tone of certainty you apply when discussing your projections or expectations for the future of a company. State your assumed replacement cycle and complement it with an acknowledgment of its variance, if appropriate.

5

QUALITY ASSURANCE

Going somewhat hand in hand with perishability and replacement cycles is the concept of quality assurance, or the importance of product and service quality.

How important is it to "get it right" the first time? Does a failure induce contractual penalties? Does it take a long time to correct the problem? Or perhaps there may only be minimal consequences, and it can be easy to get back on track after an error.

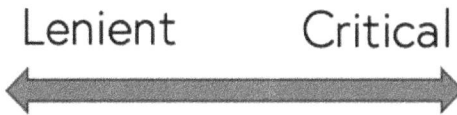

Lenient ⟵⟶ Critical

On one end of the spectrum, where the risk of an error is less relevant on a per-unit basis, we can consider restaurants, consumer goods, apparel, and other items with flexible return policies. If you asked for "no onion" on your burger, the restaurant could easily remediate the problem and bring you another burger. If that new Tshirt was a size too small, you can send it back and get the right size. In each case, the single instance of error is not enough to materially damage your perception of that particular company.[21]

On the other end of the spectrum, you could see businesses such as industrial component manufacturers, professional services firms (consultants, designers, etc.), or any B2B business that is commoditized with low switching costs. Respectively. Illustrative problems could be: poorly manufactured nuts and bolts that cause the end user device to malfunction, giving a client detrimental advice especially when advice-giving is your only line of business, or providing a faulty user experience when your solution can be readily replaced with a competitor's. A single instance of such errors could be enough to lose the customers forever in these types of businesses.

Notice that I used the qualifiers "per-unit" and "single instance" in the prior paragraphs as they highlight an important distinction. The defect scenario and its related effects on brand perception would play out differently if the negative impact were widespread through large segments of the supply chain as opposed to being confined to a single incorrect order. For context, contemplate the historical impacts of E. coli outbreaks on restaurants, or product recalls in pharmaceuticals, consumer goods, pet foods, and others.[22] Whether an issue pervades through an entire product line or manifests

---

[21] ... unless you're a "take no prisoners" perfectionist. If that were true, then good luck to all the loved ones who have to deal with you on a regular basis. ☺

[22] Visit the following Wikipedia page for some historical examples: https://en.wikipedia.org/wiki/Product_recall.

in a single instance of error is an important layer of consideration when thinking about consistency in product quality.

An additional sub-consideration in the quality assurance spectrum is the sensitivity to data breaches. While data breaches can be devastating for any firm, they are even more devastating for companies whose core selling propositions are data integrity. Cloud providers, payment card networks, and many other technology businesses cannot afford any oversight in this regard.

In sum, reflect on how likely a product or service error is for a business and how much damage (temporary and permanent) could be caused by such an error.

6

INNOVATION

The need to innovate is an important qualitative factor; some companies need to innovate often to survive, while others can move more slowly. This risk is often inversely correlated with replacement cycles. A company selling a product with a one-to-two-year replacement cycle may need to innovate more frequently than a product with a seven-to-eight-year cycle.

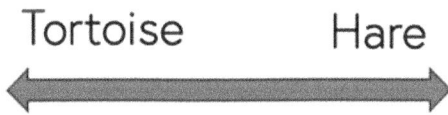

Tortoise   Hare

⟵――――――――――――――――⟶

This spectrum of innovation considers how important it is for a particular kind of business to innovate in order to maintain its competitive advantage. It is essentially a subset of a "barriers-to-entry" discussion, with frequent innovation opening the doors for new entrants. Baked within this is also an understanding around existential risk, or the distinction of a product being at risk of disappearing outright versus seeing partial softening of demand.

On one end of the spectrum, you have businesses that could be thought of as selling staples, whose demand can remain steady over a multi-year (even multi-decade) time horizon. Consider time-tested products such as a McDonald's cheeseburger, Coca-Cola, Dial soap, cardboard boxes, household tools, and natural resources, among others. Notwithstanding changes in cursory features or branding, a hammer now is not much different than a hammer from the past.

We could shift the focus slightly and expand this end of the spectrum to include assets, such as cars or houses. Now, there can be much debate around what is considered "innovative," which brings us to the following point: How you choose to define innovation is a key feature of this spectrum. Something could be innovative in function, but not design, and vice versa. Cars and houses could be thought of as being functionally constant for decades, while changing in design.

On the other end of the spectrum, you have rapidly changing industries. Fashion and apparel are prime examples, where you can't keep selling the same *exact* product for long. Consumer beauty companies have also experienced a similar effect, where a variety of small product lines have been rising in prominence at the expense of lost share from incumbents, due to ingredient innovations and novel approaches to marketing. We also commonly associate the word "innovation" with technology, for good reason; as such, certain—but not all—tech companies require agile adaptation to survive.

I alluded to how existential risk is one of the primary risks that gets teased out from the use of this innovation spectrum. Furthermore, the need to innovate also provides insight into how much the company will need to spend on R&D. And vice versa: If the amount of innovation required to compete is unclear, look at R&D

as a percentage of sales over a multi-year time horizon, and that should give you a sense.

Finally, even within slow-moving industries, there are often critical points where the innovation and technology "step" up, with those failing to make the appropriate leap falling hopelessly behind. A great example of this is the travel GDS industry, which includes Sabre, Travelport, and Amadeus. The GDS players were using mainframe transaction processing facilities originally developed in the '60s (i.e., they were using old tech). There was no real need for innovation until the emergence of OTAs (online travel agencies) like Expedia, which changed the technological demands on the intermediaries. Consequently, the three providers incorporated new technology, but they did this at different paces, which directly led to drastic shifts in market shares. Moreover, they each had differing philosophies with regard to how they approached the tech upgrade. The lesson here is that it's not only the frequency of innovation impacting an entire industry that matters, but also the timing in which individual players choose to innovate. When analyzing a company operating in the midst of industry disruption, listen to how management describes its plan to address the impending changes and compare it to the plans of competitors.

7

BUSINESS DIVERSIFICATION

The same principles that underpin portfolio diversification in investing are applicable to the "portfolios" of products or services that businesses provide. More diversity creates greater stability, lower business risk, and long-term staying power at the cost of potentially lost focus and a ceiling on explosive aggregate growth.

There are two main variables involved in assessing diversification: the quantity of items and the non-correlation of those items. In the case of a company, we can first look at the number of product or service lines it runs, in addition to the number of SKUs within those business lines. Then, we can look at any overlap in terms of product or service functions, end markets, and overall demand drivers in order to gauge correlation among the business lines.

While each variable (segment/SKU quantity and correlation) can be plotted as its own spectrum, let's merge them into an overall diversification spectrum to better illustrate this effect.

Single Product	Multiple SKUs, Single Category	Multiple, Related Categories	Multiple, Unrelated Categories

<————————————————————————————————>

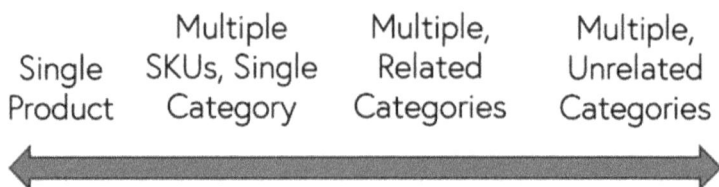

On one end of the spectrum, you have single-product companies with effectively one SKU. Consider the early stages of apps such as Uber or apparel such as Spanx. These achieved success in large part due to their relentless focus on a single idea, which also happened to be what the market really demanded. Yet countless other single-product companies fail, in part due to lack of having other performing segments to lean on when the primary product comes under pressure.

Note that many companies start out with a single-product focus and later diversify once they've achieved critical scale. In the Uber example, you could say it happened when the company came out with UberPool, UberXL, and other offerings. Though even here, we wouldn't really characterize this as a full "diversification," given that these products are all effectively different versions of the same solution.

On the spectrum, this insight brings us to the category of companies slightly inside of the single-product businesses—namely, companies with multiple SKUs but still only a single product line. An example could be a core food product with multiple flavor options. A cracker company might have sea salt, rosemary, and garlic variations, yet the core product is nevertheless a cracker. Each SKU shares the same fundamental demand drivers as the others (hungry people with a craving for salty snacks). In the case of Uber again, all the ride options essentially boil down to a fundamental desire for on-demand transportation, yet the specific options vary in terms of vehicle type or passenger density.

At the other end of the spectrum, consider multi-segment businesses. In fact, let's skim that outer edge by highlighting conglomerates who bundle practically unrelated business lines.

One such private company I covered had five distinct businesses: Risk SaaS, eLearning, quality inspection for manufacturing facilities, document publications of industry standards, and mortgage settlement services. When one business line had a bad quarter, another business often had a good quarter, and vice versa, leading to a flat and steady top line.

As with anything, there are trade-offs. Companies at this extreme are generally more stable and diversified. They are also easier to conduct strategic asset sales with, as an asset divestiture should have minimal impact on the rest of the businesses. However, the fact that the disparate business lines share few features in common makes integrating them under one parent more difficult, leading to fewer cost-saving, cross-selling, and other synergistic opportunities. In other words, the economies of scale effects are dampened compared to those in single-product firms that generate the same dollar amount of revenues.

Back toward the middle-right of the spectrum we can put companies that have multiple product lines that are at least somewhat correlated. You might say this is a cost-benefit sweet spot. A beverage company like Coca-Cola not only has its flagship soda products but also juices, sports drinks, and waters. Additionally, a tech company like Apple provides phones, laptops, watches, and more. The product lines are relatable enough to create synergies, yet their target markets vary enough to provide benefits of diversity. A firm lying in between the company profiles mentioned in the prior paragraph could be Johnson & Johnson. You could also consider a specialty chemical conglomerate, such as Element Solutions. Each company's various products appear unrelated, yet they share some manufacturing and sales processes (allowing for some synergies and realization of scale advantages), in addition to similar high-level macroeconomic forces.

Two more examples are called for, as they clearly demonstrate hedging effects from separate lines of business.

The first is the business model of a mortgage servicing company, which often also includes an originations business. The servicing segment makes money by charging a fee percentage on unpaid principal balance (UPB). The originations segment generates cash by effectively charging a spread on loans originated. In other words, total servicing fees will increase as UPB increases, and total origination revenues increase as origination volumes increase. Where does the "hedge" come into play? If interest rates fall, mortgage prepayment rates will rise, reducing UPB (leading to lost revenue for the mortgage servicer) but increasing mortgage origination volumes (boosting origination revenues). Conversely, if interest rates rise, UPB attrition will slow, yet mortgage originations will fall, all else being equal.

The second is a specific power generation portfolio I once underwrote. Two of the plants—one coal plant and one gas plant—

functioned together as a synthetic hedge. If gas prices would fall, the spark spread and capacity factor of the gas plant would increase, which would offset lower power prices. If gas prices would rise, the capacity factor of the gas plant would come down, but the portfolio would benefit from higher power prices as well as higher dark spreads due to a reversal of coal-to-gas-switching.[23]

MIX SHIFT IMPACTS

Most of this discussion has revolved around revenue impacts, but the same can hold true for costs. Furthermore, it's critically important to think about margin differentials and multi-segment companies' profit sensitivity to mix shifts. Say company A has two segments, each generating a 40% margin. Company B has two segments: One generates a 20% margin and the other generates a 60% margin. With each company, one segment sees revenues rise, and the other sees revenues decline in similar proportion. The margins for company A will stay the same, whereas company B's will experience a mix shift, pushing profitability either up or down, depending on whether the high-margin or low-margin business is experiencing the growth.

The impact of mix shift is an extremely common factor discussed on earnings calls. There are many situations where overall revenues are up year over year, yet EBITDA is down (and vice versa), with the

---

[23] Don't worry about the industry jargon in this example if you don't understand it. The high-level explanation is that per-unit margins would fluctuate inversely with volumes.

explanation being mix shift. From an analysis perspective, you would be wise to treat each individual segment as its own business. Project separate revenue growth and margin trajectories while making some assumption on shared SG&A,[24] provided you have the information.

---

[24] From a modeling perspective, this would look like having a sum of the parts revenue with a similar setup for COGS (where each segment's COGS is based on a percentage of sales for that segment's revenue). Then for your SG&A, you can calculate that as a percentage of total sales.

8

DIFFERENTIATION

(COMMODITIZATION VS. SPECIALIZATION)

Every business solution can be considered a commodity that's readily replaceable, a specialized offering with key differentiating features, or something in between. All else being equal, it's better to offer a differentiated product than a commodity, as far as business risk goes.

Commodity   Specialty

$$\longleftrightarrow$$

Still, plenty of companies can get by without having differentiated products—in fact, many industries are formed exclusively around commodities, including metals & mining, power generation, and energy.

A useful example where this spectrum explicitly comes into play is in the case of a chemicals company. On one end of the spectrum, the company may be providing a commoditized, low value–added product, such as fertilizer, titanium dioxide, or polymer. This segment is classified as basic chemicals. On the other end, you have (as the name would fit) specialty chemicals, which include adhesives, coatings, and additives.

There are relative trade-offs between the two categories. A commodity company will generally have lower margins and a lower EV multiple than its specialty counterpart. Commodity companies will compete more heavily on marginal production cost and scale, where utilization and capacity factors are critical. Yet commodity products will usually have broader applications and a larger market to sell into compared to the highly specific (yet sticky) focus of specialty companies.

Of course, this commoditization filter can be applied to a wide variety of industries. "*What makes your product different?*" is a staple question for consumer products companies. You can even see this dynamic play out in the case of value-add resellers (VARs) or distributors: A commoditized distributor purely moves product and skims a margin, whereas other categories of distributors provide more value through additional maintenance and specialized consulting services.

As an interesting middle-ground example, consider the bottled water industry. Water is a commodity, right? Yet, we would say a bottle of Icelandic is much different than a bottle of Dasani. Certain items, which start out as commodities, can be modified within the consumer's mind and differentiated to a point of relevant specialization. To discuss strategies for product differentiation more in depth is outside the scope of this book, but at the very least you can see how branding, with its packaging and associated stories, can influence this variable.

In sum, the designation of commodity vs. specialty effectively channels the relevance of the question: What makes your product or service better than that of your competitors? If it's not different, can it be made different? And if not, as is the case of many commoditized industries, what about the operations of the business is meaningfully different from that of its competitors?

9

SECRET SAUCE

There is a tug-of-war between an investor's desire to know every little detail around a company's operations and a company's desire to limit information disclosure and protect its trade secrets.

As such, beyond what is required from a regulatory perspective, most management teams will only disclose just enough information to placate investors and get a deal done.

The secret sauce spectrum measures this element of undiscoverable[25] ambiguity surrounding a business model, in addition to the level of trust in management that is required to offset this.

---

[25] Oftentimes, the information to understand a business model is actually available, but many of the investors still don't understand it, and there will be an associated risk premium to compensate for this. The complexity risk premium becomes very attractive for the investor that can navigate such nuances effectively.

Transparent   Opaque

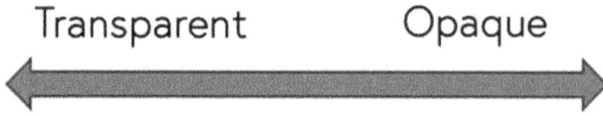

A clear example of this principle is found among the market-making/high frequency trading firms, which include Virtu, Citadel Securities, Jane Street, Hudson River Trading, and DRW. These companies generate income by posting bids and offers on various securities, capturing the associated spread.

How do they determine which prices to present to the market? These firms use proprietary algorithms along with exabytes' (if not petabytes') worth of data. As an analyst, you don't get to see these algorithms or this data, making this kind of firm's business model a "black box." Still, plenty of people get comfortable with these investments despite the reservation of not knowing the "secret sauce."

This category of "secret sauce" can alternatively be classified as a dependency on intellectual property (IP), which you might measure as a percentage of total assets.

Companies toward this end of the spectrum might include software, consulting, specialty manufacturing, and niche servicers. The main point is that you know the company is generating sales, but you're not sure exactly *how* they produce their good or service, even after conducting a value chain analysis (See *Value-Add Spectrum*).

What type of factors should an investor lean on when confronted with such a situation? At the very least, there should be a convincing track record of sales or product efficacy (e.g., studies and research in the case of a biotech or pharma product). The longer the company has been around, the more you can trust their process. If the offered solution can be modified with minimal business disruption, as in the prior case of a market-making/trading strategy, then there should exist adequate risk controls, incentives for management consistency, or any other barriers preventing drastic change in the production process.

The other end of the secret sauce spectrum is self-explanatory, entailing the kinds of products and services that are easily understandable, with an independently verifiable value proposition.

Consider the example of a screw. There is no real secret to its manufacturing process (metal in a molding), and its application can be readily tested by outside parties.

To summarize, if a company has a "secret sauce" (IP), this could be good for sustainable competitive advantage, yet it could potentially increase the perceived risk of the investment (since you don't really know what's happening under the hood or what exactly makes the sauce a "secret").

NATURE
OF
REVENUE

10

REVENUE VISIBILITY

Visibility is a critical feature of a company's revenue stream. The company may be receiving revenue today, but how much assurance does it have of revenue to come in the future? How far in advance and with how much precision can management confidently predict sales?

Zero Lead Time   Contractually Guaranteed
                                      Revenue, Years Out

$$\longleftrightarrow$$

On one end of the spectrum, you have low-visibility businesses that rely on point-in-time orders placed with zero lead time. On the other end of the spectrum, you have businesses that have revenues formed around stable contracts with specified pricing and volumes over time. Of course, one would prefer more visibility compared to less, all else being equal.

An archetypal example of the former is an average tech hardware business. After an initial product purchase, the consumer may not need to upgrade for a long time and may unexpectedly keep delaying such future purchases. In this category, I am also reminded of a business model like that of a components manufacturer supplying consumer electronics companies with specific parts with only four-to-six weeks' notice. A third example would be a service provider whose demand is tied to infrastructure projects that are repeatedly exposed to regulatory delays. These companies deal with unexpected orders and are more likely to report "surprises."

On the opposite side of the spectrum, where future revenue visibility is very high, you could see setups such as a power generation plant with a multi-year PPA (power purchase agreement) covering most of its capacity. You could also consider an asset management firm with locked-up capital, whereby the firm earns a percentage fee on AUM ratably throughout the year.

Somewhere in the middle we might consider a subscription-based business that auto-bills monthly with an option for the consumer to opt out each period. The consumer can cancel their subscription at a moment's notice, yet the force of inertia[26] (or breakage in certain cases) can provide minor assurance in some sort of revenue base, as quantified by historical retention rates.

You might even group in businesses whose transactions have low guaranteed visibility, yet have practical reliability, such as in the case of restaurants or retail stores. It's unlikely for the restaurant's or grocery

---

[26] Consider the effects of the status quo and conservatism biases, in addition to the persuasion principle of commitment.

store's volumes to disappear overnight, despite their nonexistent lead times. In these cases, the high frequency nature of the transaction counts as a mitigating effect to the low visibility, but we'll save this feature for the next chapter.

In contrast with the low-visibility businesses, the high-visibility businesses generally have fewer instances of selling activities, by virtue of nailing down longer-term contracts (as opposed to a onetime sale). This framework conceptually covers the recurring vs. non-recurring revenue split as well, which is among the most common ways management breaks down revenue.[27]

The visibility spectrum can further be thought of as a measurement for the risk of an earnings surprise (whether positive or negative), which ultimately translates to a security's short-term market price volatility. This volatility, of course, can work both ways, not only exposing you to unexpected downside, but giving you opportunities for demand upside or acceleration (which might otherwise be prevented from locked-in contracts or hedges).

A final distinction to be made is related to the source of that visibility (or lack thereof). Are we talking about demand-side visibility or supply-side visibility? The examples above focused more on the demand side—namely, the unexpected timing for when a consumer decides to walk in the door, pick up the phone, or log in online to place their order. With regard to supply-side visibility, think about risks of bottlenecks in the supply chain. Does the product need to go

---

[27] This is typically how management will signal its revenue visibility. Analysts will actively look for this "recurring" revenue language in the company materials or ask for it in Q&A if it's missing.

through various regulatory approvals and certifications? Are the manufacturing partners consistent in their delivery schedules? How smooth and reliable is the overall production process?

11

REVENUE LUMPINESS

Often considered hand in hand with visibility, revenue lumpiness is another critical feature of a business's revenue stream. The "lumpiness" effectively refers to transaction- or order-size concentration, which can be quantified as the average transaction dollar amount as a percentage of the total sales.

A Few Large Transactions   Millions of Small Transactions

$$\longleftrightarrow$$

On one end of the spectrum, you have businesses whose total sales can be distinctly derived from only a handful of individual chunks or transactions. On the other end, you would see businesses whose total revenues are aggregated up from millions of relatively small individual transactions.

In the case of the former, lumpy businesses might resemble those that are heavily project-based, perhaps tied to some sort of construction activity. There are also low-volume equipment manufacturers, such as those who produce mail inserters and sorters. But perhaps most appropriately, we can really be thinking about lumpiness more universally, in the sense that most businesses (regardless of industry) start out lumpy by design. In other words, a new business may only have one or two contracts compared to its mature competitor, which has hundreds of contracts. Try to differentiate between this kind of "new company" lumpiness and the kind of lumpiness that would be present even in a mature company's business model.

Conversely, on the other side of it, we see businesses that don't live and die by the status of a single order. In fact, their revenues would hardly flinch at the loss of any particular transaction. The examples of restaurants and retail stores come to mind again; the loss of one transaction may only represent a 0.00001% decline in total revenue. Similarly, you can include other types of platform-based businesses, who see remarkably high volumes of transactions or users flowing through their pipes. Thirdly, let's not forget the payment processors who support much of these other businesses. After paying the interchange fees, the merchant acquirer may only keep $0.50 for every $100 a consumer spends, yet the insanely high number of volumes processed aggregate up to hundreds of millions of dollars in sales for these firms.

Not unlike in the case of revenue visibility, revenue lumpiness creates greater volatility, where the scale of the business can vary drastically from period to period, compared to non-lumpy businesses whose revenues might only move +/- 2–3% in any given period.

12

CLIENT CONCENTRATION - INDIVIDUAL

Related to revenue lumpiness that is based on transactions, we have the important factor of client concentration. Here we would ask, how many clients does the company have? How is the company's revenue distributed among these clients? Is there a heavy reliance on a particular client? What percentage of revenue does the top client represent? How about the top five? The top ten? And so on.

Naturally, the more concentrated a company is, the less negotiating leverage it has, with substantial power going to the buyer.

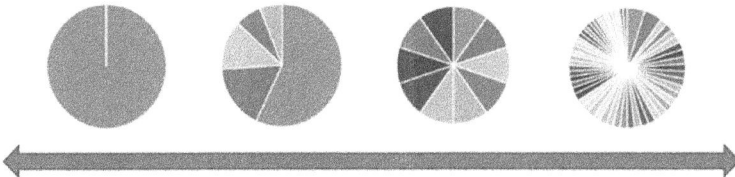

On one end of the spectrum, you have companies that have only one primary customer. Unless you're at a VC evaluating startups, this is less common, so perhaps a more practical representation of an "extreme" would be to think about companies who have one client representing more than 50% of revenues.

On the other end of the spectrum, you have businesses with diversified customer bases, where no customer represents more than 1% of revenue (you could even set the threshold lower than that, depending on the types of companies you spend time thinking about).

As far as industries are concerned, some have customer concentration by design. The main example I would provide is in the case of companies dealing with the large mobile network operators (AT&T, Verizon, Sprint, etc.). If you are a telco services company providing a B2B solution to a market that only has a handful of players, then inevitably your revenues will be concentrated.[28] In other words, within a particular product or service, you cannot be more diversified than the addressable market itself. So we can readily lump into this "concentrated" category any other B2B solutions providers that serve market oligopolies.

When looking at a company with client concentration, some otherwise secondary considerations begin to rise in prominence. In discussing their top client, management may point to the fact that within this client are many individual contracts, each which represent much smaller portions of revenue (i.e., that in reality there is great diversity within this initial appearance of concentration). They may also

---

[28] If you are serving a market with only five players, then the best diversification you could ever achieve is one with five customers.

point to the long tenure with that customer, or to some other characteristics as evidence for the strength in the relationship. In other words, if you have identified that a company has client concentration, investigate further to determine the quality of the relationship in addition to whether there are sub-contracts within that relationship.

This brings us to follow-up considerations for companies that lack customer concentration (or, positively phrased, companies with customer diversification), which will be covered next in the sections on end-market and channel mixes. But at a high level, the point here is that if the company has a diversified customer base, then you should consider correlations among the demand behaviors of that customer base. You may have 1,000 clients, but if 200 of them will act effectively in lockstep, then you still have a concentration issue, albeit in a slightly different manner.

13

CLIENT CONCENTRATION - ENDMARKET

As a next step in thinking about customer diversification, it's important to consider potential correlations found among the company's various clients. Such correlations are most commonly derived from shared industries, and thus being aware of a company's end-market breakdown becomes vital. Which industries do the company's clients participate in? What are the associated risks within those industries, and how might they affect the client's purchasing behaviors? Do these risks offset each other by virtue of end-market diversification?

On one end of the spectrum, you have businesses whose clients all originate from the *same* industry. If something hits the overall industry, the company could be crushed due to its industry concentration. As before, this end can include B2B service providers who provide a very niche solution, only applicable to certain industries. In such instances, you should, of course, look for an added risk premium on the investment's rate of return.

On the other end of the spectrum, you have businesses with a vast array of end markets (you could say, for example, that no individual industry represents more than 10% of sales). Here you would look at the top industry exposures and apply yours or your firm's current industry outlook as a filter for setting business expectations.

These end-market considerations tend to flare up when there are acute, industry-specific shocks. Investors experienced this in the 2015 Energy crisis, where "What's this company's exposure to Energy?" became a staple question in due diligence. We saw similar attitudes toward retail in subsequent years in light of rising e-commerce trends, and in the midst of COVID-19 occurring at the time of this writing, we are seeing concerns of a similar nature with regard to travel, hospitality, and restaurant end-market exposures.

To sum up thus far, how relevant this spectrum is to your analysis depends first upon whether there is end-market concentration. If the industry exposures are diversified, then I recommend sizing the share of topical or problematic sectors (i.e., "What's this company's exposure to Retail/Energy/etc.?"). Perhaps you want the company to have zero exposure to any "undesirable" sectors.

Additionally, you may garner that this spectrum is more commonly applicable to B2B business models as opposed to B2C. A client base formed around individual consumers will inherently be more diversified (because there are more people than there are businesses); plus, the concept of a consumer being tied to an "end market" may strike some as a category error. In this B2C case, the end-market filter might be better understood as looking at which end markets are responsible for employing the consumer base. For something like fast casual restaurants, end-market concentration is effectively irrelevant, as your store will have consumers coming from all sorts of employers and backgrounds. But if you are looking at a B2C company like a pool supplies retailer, the end-market filter retains some relevance, as you think, for example, about housing construction (new-build and renovation) or correlations to other industry-specific trends. In other words, the pool supplies retailer could be said to have end-market concentration in the housing market.

To recap, identify the "pie chart" of end-market exposure, analyzing relative shares, and also look for any topical or problematic industries. Explore the trade-off of investing in a company that is concentrated in one "good" end market vs. a company that is more diversified in its end markets yet serves a few of the "topical" or undesirable industries.

14

CLIENT CONCENTRATION - CHANNEL

Within this discussion of correlations among consumers, it is also worth discussing channel mix, or the variety of distribution paths a company uses to reach its consumers. There are many ways to categorize sales channels, and some of the common labels are direct-to-consumer, retail, wholesale, e-commerce, brokerage, independent sales organizations, direct mail, and others.

Diving into the specific structure of every distribution channel is outside the scope of this discussion, and the basic ideas for these can be understood with a few brief web searches. Rather, here the framing will be on channel diversification.

While it's generally rare for an entire channel to become existentially questionable, the recent secular declines of retail have elevated the topic of channel diversification into greater prominence. Furthermore, increased channel diversification might allow a company greater ability to negotiate pricing and maximize its marketing ROI, provided it doesn't lose strategic focus.

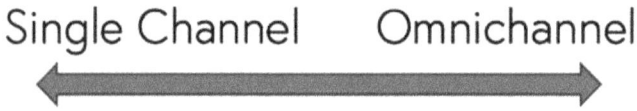

Single Channel   Omnichannel

$$\longleftrightarrow$$

On one end of the spectrum, we see companies with a single go-to-market path. This can include e-commerce/DTC-only consumer products. You could even lump in MLM/direct selling firms such as Herbalife, Rodan + Fields, or Amway. Studying examples in the latter category perhaps best illustrates channel risk, as many MLMs are notorious for being short-lived due to their inherent inability to pivot into other channels once the businesses mature.

On the other end of the spectrum, you have firms with—to use the management buzzword—"omnichannel" marketing. These businesses incorporate a mixed combination of online and physical locations, in addition to an active sales force. A diverse channel mix allows for more pathways to both existing and incremental customers, in addition to providing strategic maneuverability. Of course, the downsides of such features are greater expenses and administrative burdens.

Some firms will show "multiple" channels by slicing up a single, broad vertical. For example, a company might sell exclusively through retail (i.e., a single channel), yet stratify the pie into "big-box" stores, local independents, and specialty retailers. These distinctions add value, but make sure you determine whether the categories should actually be considered separate channels from a supply-chain, selling, and general risk perspective. In other words, you should consider viewing these channels on a more consolidated basis, since the company's presentation of diversification may be misleading (or it's a diversification measured by irrelevant attributes).

Before concluding, it's worth highlighting a sub-spectrum within the online sales channel, given the prevalence of e-commerce businesses. This spectrum centers upon fulfillment and distribution strategies, and I would bucket it into four categories.

1) An e-commerce company can go directly to the consumer (DTC), selling from its own website and shipping from its own warehouses.

2) The company can send its inventory to Amazon (or others like it), who will display the product and also fulfill the logistics and delivery.

3) The merchant can sell on Amazon as in #2 but handle fulfillment internally via shipment of goods to customers.

4) A retailer can buy inventory from the merchant and assume all of the risk in selling. (Of course, this traditional path is present outside of online channels.)

Naturally, these options involve trade-offs of risks, convenience, and economics. At any given point in time, one strategy may be preferable to another.

Returning to the broader point, it's ultimately up to you to assess the efficacy of the company's specific channels and marketing strategies. The spectrum here provides the first step in bringing your awareness to what those channels are.

15

CUSTOMER TENURE AND REASONS FOR LEAVING

Furthering the focus on the nature of customers, we come to the category of customer tenure and the reasons for ending a commercial relationship.

"Long-standing relationships" is an incredibly common marketing point trotted out by management (and such a feature is afforded to more mature companies by definition), though it's not without good reason. Humans generally have a bias toward commitment and consistency and would prefer to continue doing what has worked for them in the past, all else being equal. In a sense you could say that customers you've had for a long time will give you more leniency and greater margin for error than new customers; hence the concept of "customer acquisition cost."[29]

---

[29] In terms of marketing and advertising, it costs incrementally more to gain the trust and loyalty of a new customer than it does to keep one who is already familiar with your services.

On one end of the spectrum, you have companies with customer relationships spanning at least a decade (if not more). At the very least, such relationships tell you that someone out there has found the value proposition of the business being analyzed compelling. In fact, they have continued to find it compelling over many years and have known the solution provider long enough to see through any short-term sales gimmicks.

Stated alternatively, long-standing relationships give you confidence that the concept is more than proven and that there is some "real" business here. It could also signal to you the sustainability of that portion of the business, but it would be prudent not to generalize too much, given that businesses with long-standing relationships are also susceptible to being existentially displaced.

On the other end of the spectrum are companies having customers with no particular loyalty—they are here today and gone tomorrow. This could be a commoditized product business whose customer base is comprised of individual consumers making onetime purchases. For many such consumer businesses (particularly those with subscription models), the concepts of lifetime value

("LTV"), retention, and attrition curves become valuable, so you could get a sense of the average tenure and profitability associated with their representative customer.

As alluded to earlier, this low-tenure category could technically include any early-stage business, which simply hasn't been around long enough to have "long-term" relationships with its customers. In these cases, it becomes even more important to evaluate the overall quality of the relationship and the specific touch points between the two parties.

Another mitigant for lack of customer tenure is the depth and breadth of entrenchment present within a business–client relationship. In other words, consider the "switching costs," or the degree to which it's cumbersome for a customer to unplug from the existing business and get its needs met elsewhere. The greater the switching costs, the less likely a client will go with a competitor, and the more relative value a competitor would have to bring in order to win that client away.

We already know that a loss of a large client should immediately spark a red flag for further investigation. The same is true for loss of a long-tenured customer (though, admittedly, the two features of size and tenure are correlated). In these cases, it is very important to ascertain why customers leave. Is it due to your company making a misstep? Did the competitor do something better? Perhaps something completely out of the company's control happened. Can the customer be won back? If so, how long might it take to win them back, and how costly might that be?

The spectrum with regard to reasons for leaving can be plotted as one of circumstances in a company's control compared to those that are not.

It's not you. It's me.   It's you.

On one end, we see the worst reason, which is when a company has fundamentally failed at delivering on its value position (see more in the *Quality Assurance* chapter).

On the other end, we see external reasons that lie beyond the company's control. Most commonly this could look like a customer getting acquired (M&A) or going bankrupt. Somewhere in the middle we would find situations like a customer achieving scale and deciding to insource. Ideally, your hope (should management provide the information) is that the company being at fault as a reason for leaving is rare (representing, say, <10% of customers lost).[30]

---

[30] If you're looking at certain distressed or turnaround situations, you could make an alternative case that if prior management was at fault, that actually provides greater opportunity to fix the business and restore enterprise value than if the loss of customers was arbitrary. Of course, the ability to win back the trust of customers (and implement related strategies) then becomes critical.

16

ENTERPRISE VS. SMB

Generally speaking, a company's clients are either other businesses or individual consumers. Stated alternatively, most companies operate either B2B or B2C models.[31] In the B2B space, we have already discussed determining the end markets of those clients. Additionally, it is important to ascertain the relative scale and sophistication of those clients. With regard to the continuum framing of this book, here we have a spectrum of SMBs, SMEs, and large enterprises.

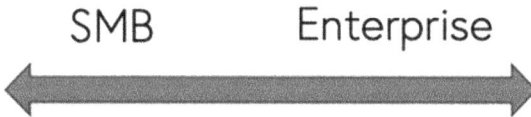

SMB   Enterprise

On one end of the spectrum, we find small- to medium-sized businesses. This includes the local mom & pops and companies that typically have one primary point of presence. On the other end of

---

[31] I considered devoting a separate section to this topic, but the B2B vs. B2C distinction is not really a spectrum. Rather, it's a fairly binary designation.

the spectrum, we have large enterprises, including all of the blue-chip names the average person would be familiar with, such as Microsoft, Apple, Google, and Amazon. In the middle of this spectrum, we would place small- to medium-sized enterprises. As far as where the lines get drawn for these classifications, they will vary depending upon legal jurisdiction or management's discretion. But for our purposes, you can consider the SMEs to be those with 100–500 employees or $10–$100m in revenues.

Qualitatively, the small businesses differ from the large enterprises in terms of sheer number, sales approach, relative stability, and level of sophistication.

As one would expect, the number of small businesses that exist far outweighs the number of large enterprises. In the US, you could call it 15 million of the former and 15,000 of the latter. Practically speaking, a business targeting SMBs will have more relationships to manage and more sales leads to pursue. Conversely, the larger clients will typically provide you more volumes but with pricing concessions.

In the case of SMB customers, it might be easier for the B2B provider to win new clients as decision-making tends to occur faster in smaller organizations. There is also the distinction of making a localized sale at a particular office compared to engaging in dialogue with a regional head responsible for multiple locations.

Differentials of business stability also come into play when comparing organizations of varying scale. Default rates and bankruptcies are much higher for SMBs. For a B2B provider servicing SMBs, this will naturally result in a higher churn rate, typically around 20% for its SMB clients. This churn factor also translates into lower average relationship tenure.

Fourthly, the level of sophistication and expertise tends to vary substantially between the SMB and large enterprise categories. The SMB clients may require more education with regard to the B2B provider's value-proposition. Yet with the large enterprises, there is a greater risk of these firms deciding to insource and develop their own in-house solutions.

The SMB-enterprise spectrum applies to many industries. Notable examples where this topic arises include merchant acquirers, value-add resellers, SaaS companies, and other software and services providers. Again, churn rates become a key consideration, in addition to margin differentials per client.

In sum, if the company you are analyzing sells to other businesses, determine where these clients fall on the SMB-enterprise spectrum and consider the associated risks.

17

SALES CYCLE AND CUSTOMER ACQUISITION

Ideas related to selling activities have already been interspersed throughout the various sections, but it's worth giving the sales cycle its own set of spectrums, too. Three of the more common considerations that arise here are time-to-market, seasonality, and customer acquisition.

Time-to-market ("TTM") has been implicitly addressed in the *Innovation Spectrum* chapter,[32] as the required speed to market and risk of innovation in an industry tend to go hand in hand. On one side, you could maximize speed to market in order to mitigate the effects of innovation from new entrants. But this can come at the risk of introducing issues of quality control and potential loss of strategic focus. On the other end, you could take your time and be more

---

[32] It has also been implied in the *Revenue Visibility* section, in terms of product lead times and how far in advance of the sale that the selling activities need to commence.

strategic, at the risk of being left behind by your competition. The sweet spot along this line is less of an absolute, and more about matching what the industry of your business requires.

Aside from such cases of technological disruption, the concept of TTM can also be applied to businesses where logistics are paramount. As an example, consider the business of a sodium cyanide (NaCN) manufacturer. Gold miners use this commodity chemical to facilitate the extraction of gold from the rest of the mined rock. In this case, whether the NaCN manufacturer wins the contract has a lot to do with the geographic proximity of the chemical plant to the mining site—this is a "speed"-to-market issue in its most literal and concrete sense. Logistics are important to every business, but for some they are the central driver of revenue.

Seasonality, when it exists,[33] often becomes a critical component in the riskiness of a business. To be clear, we are referring to the temporal distribution of product or service sales throughout the year. Do most of the yearly sales come in one quarter, or are the revenues spread evenly throughout the year?

---

[33] ... exists meaningfully, that is. You'll never see a business with a perfectly uniform distribution of sales, getting 25% of annual sales in Q1, 25% in Q2, and so on. So, one might claim seasonality exists in every business. Yet it's also important to differentiate between predictable seasonality and random quarterly variance. In other words, for seasonality to "exist" in a way that can be analyzed, it must be the case that, for example, each year Q3s will be higher/lower than Q2s (adjusted for any stepwise shocks to the business). You can also look for situations where some businesses operate negative EBITDA for a quarter or two and then have a massive positive swing in another quarter, consistently each year.

Seasonality comes in all sorts of flavors. There is the consumer-led seasonality tied to specific holidays and events, such as Christmas or back-to-school shopping. Perhaps the best demonstration of consumer-driven seasonality is in floral businesses, where half of revenues come from Valentine's Day and Mother's Day. Other common examples of seasonality include CRE leasing and housing cycles, and B2B sales tied to seasonal IT spend. There is also the category of seasonality related to the actual *seasons*, or weather patterns, affecting businesses such as power generation peaker plants, disaster repair and recovery servicers, and construction companies.

The sub-spectrum here would be high seasonality vs. low seasonality. Or we can dub it a spectrum of "temporal concentration," or lumping.[34] To further highlight the high end of the spectrum, consider the case of a leading K–12 travel organization. This company provides educational summer trips to Washington, DC, among other locations. Customers will put down deposits 9–12 months in advance of the trip, and the company doesn't have to pay out flight and hotel vendors until the trip is only a few weeks away. The gap between the timing of cash receipts and delivery of the product & service creates substantial deferred revenue. The company gets the cash up front but also must recognize it as a liability until it delivers the service and earns that revenue. In other words, if the service isn't going to be delivered, the cash will have to be returned. COVID-19 triggered the

---

[34] Questions to ask: Are the annual sales lumped into one period each year? If all of the bookings for the year happen in one quarter, and something bad happens that quarter, will the company have to wait 12 months to make the next sale? Or can they recover faster and chalk it up to a "delay" or lag in sales?

worst-case scenario: The summer trips were canceled, and the company had to refund $300m of cash, which it no longer had, ripping up the fabric of the business model. To make matters worse, customers were reticent to put new deposits down for the 2021 summer trip, meaning that expectations for any operating cash inflows were indefinitely postponed. This is an extreme case, but it highlights key risks found in seasonal gaps between cash inflows and outflows, in addition to how the damage in disrupted seasonal businesses can take longer to repair compared to their non-seasonal counterparts.

The third sub-spectrum to cover is the method of customer acquisition. On one hand, you have cold calling of specific individuals and other forms of direct outreach. On the other hand, you look at paid advertising that's meant to attract a wide base of viewers. In other words, the sales strategy of the business will fall somewhere between "You come to the customer" vs. "The customer comes to you." Which strategy is more effective can vary for many reasons, but at the very least it should inform how management allocates marketing spend. Do they spend on advertising campaigns to lure in the customer, or do they rely on a direct selling effort supported by a sales force? Consider the differences between how one might encounter the products of Nike compared to those of Herbalife.[35]

---

[35] One will likely see a Nike product in a commercial, whereas an MLM product like Herbalife will be presented to the customer by an active sales representative. In the context of this topic, one could also consider the differences between push and pull marketing, but such nuance exceeds the scope of practical investment risk analysis. In other words, "This is a solid company, but the use of pull marketing will be its downfall," is something you are unlikely to ever hear in an investment committee.

In sum, try to understand the timing of the company's sales cycle, its seasonality, and its balance of selling vs. marketing activities.

18

WALLET SHARE

When a business sells to a customer with a specific need, it's important to consider what that business's wallet share is with that customer. In other words, determine what percentage of a customer's total purchases in a particular category is made with the business being analyzed. Is the customer purchasing different brands of the same product or allocating all of that category spend to one vendor? Is a company sole-sourcing or multi-sourcing? Wallet share can also be thought of as an inverse of supplier concentration.[36]

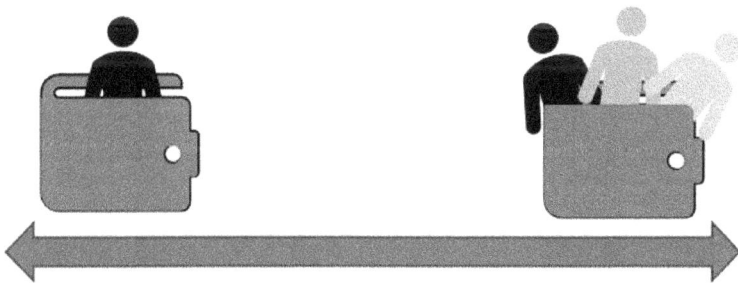

---

[36] E.g., if you equally allocate your supplier spend among three suppliers, each supplier resents 33% of that spend. From any of these suppliers' perspective, they have 33% of your wallet share.

On one end of the spectrum, we consider customers who engage in sole-sourcing, where they'll fulfill their entire needs with one vendor. Here we may also see contracts based on mutual exclusivity. Elements of trust and product quality become paramount in such scenarios, given that the customer is fully reliant upon the one business for a particular need. Consequently, the sales processes here might also entail more diligence and RFP-like structures.

On the other end, we can find clients with diverse purchase orders, multi-sourcing from a variety of vendors. Generally speaking, sourcing from multiple vendors will give a customer more negotiating leverage when it comes to pricing. However, there may be more G&A needed to maintain the greater number of relationships in addition to logistical considerations. Additionally, sales process might be of the order-filling, on-demand kind here.

When it comes to the size of average wallet share for a business you're analyzing, bigger is usually better, with preference toward your company being the customer's sole provider of the particular solution rather than being one of many.[37] If the client sources from both your business and other competitors, then the next consideration is whether your business is the leading supplier for that customer, and what the relative shares and orderings among the various players are.

---

[37] This kind of scenario, along with features like mutual exclusivity, is naturally more applicable to B2B businesses as opposed to B2C. In the B2C case, it's a matter of how you frame the category. For example, your company's protein bar might be the only brand a particular consumer buys (=100% wallet share); however, it might be one of many nutrition bars that customer buys (<100% wallet share).

Wallet share is most useful when comparing a business's product or service to comparable or substitutable solutions at a fungible level of specificity. By way of example, if you are a bicycle manufacturer, it is useful to know what share of bikes in your consumer's garage your bike represents. It is not as useful to say, for example, "Our bike is the only red mountain bike with clip-in pedals in the customer's garage," which is overly specific. The alternative, broadening case is to compare that customer's total dollar spend on bikes versus total transportation spend (including cars, Uber rides, etc.). While such conceptual broadening has its own worthwhile utility and strategic value, it is too generalized for the purposes of the traditional "wallet share" assessment.

There is another variant of wallet share that is worth mentioning, though it is not recognized as such.[38] It comes primarily in the case of industrial manufacturing, or a business that supplies a part to someone who combines it with other parts to make a whole product. Consider the example of a component producer for smartphones. Let's say that this manufacturer produces a display driver (a small metal, chip-like piece that is inside the phone) for the phone. Management of such a company might say: "Our component represents only $2 of this $900 phone." What is so good about mentioning this fact? I thought bigger share is always better? Well, the executives would be quick in telling you that this low share of total product cost

---

[38] It's not exactly "wallet share," but I prefer to include this discussion here, rather than separating it out. Actual wallet share in the example given would deal with determining if the client sources from multiple providers of smartphone display drivers.

suggests that pricing pressure from the client is unlikely. The implied notion is: What's the point of actively negotiating the $2 down to $1.75, if that barely moves the needle on the total price?[39] Yet some companies do engage in squeezing even the smallest of suppliers, so one should always be wary in embracing that line from management.

In conclusion, being a primary or sole provider for a client will be better than not. Determine the business's wallet share, see how much the shares have shifted around over time, and uncover the reasons driving such shifts.

Thus far, we've discussed concentration in terms of sources of revenue; in the next couple of sections, we'll think about factors pertaining to costs.

---

[39] If you were reading this point critically, you would have caught that the $2 being contrasted with the $900 is a faulty comparison, assuming that the $900 is referring to the retail price. It should be compared to the unit manufacturing cost.

NATURE
OF
EXPENSES

19

SUPPLIER CONCENTRATION

Similar in its relevance to revenues, the factor of concentration applies to costs as well, with supplier concentration being the analogue to customer concentration. We have also already mentioned how supplier concentration and wallet share are essentially two sides of the same coin.

On one side of the spectrum, you have companies sourcing from only one supplier, whereas, on the other side you have companies with diversified supplier bases.

In the former case, primary risks include a disadvantaged bargaining position and greater potential for supply chain disruption. The supplier may be able to eat into more of the company's gross margin (compared to what the market average would be), and the company could also see massive delays if any operating issues arise with the supplier. To mitigate such concentration, you could inquire as to whether there are long-term contracts in place that specify steady terms on pricing and provide for sub-contracting provisions, or some sort of backup optionality in the event of a failure to deliver.

In the latter case, we see the benefit of diversity, which offsets the aforementioned bargaining and supply chain risks. However, the cost of this diversity entails more resources dedicated to managing these relationships, in addition to potentially greater logistical complexities. There also exists a practical ceiling to achieving diversity, whereby larger suppliers can take greater orders at better unit economics, incentivizing a company to replace its multiple small vendors with a single vendor who can handle the larger load.

As a final point, it's worth mentioning that, similar to the case of other spectrums, you can contextualize the concept of supplier concentration across various points along the value chain. "Supplier" can refer not only to a raw materials or components provider but also a wholesaler or distributor. Regardless of the designation, the principles of bargaining power, risk diversification, and unit economics are the same.

20

RAW MATERIALS CONCENTRATION

Where applicable, a company's mix of raw materials is very relevant. The analysis here is like the other spectrums of concentration, particularly the end-market concentration.

At the initial glance, we apply the standard concentration spectrum framework: On one end you have companies relying on a single raw material, whereas, on the other end you have companies with a diversified base of raw materials. As is typical, greater diversity contributes more stability to the financials. Beyond this primary layer, there are two additional features to consider.

First, one should identify the features and trends of the relevant raw material's pricing. How volatile has it been? Is it fairly stochastic? What is its price correlated with?[40] Of course, more volatility translates into more risk. Applying this variable to the context of our

---

[40] For many raw materials, there will be some correlation to oil prices, as an example. You can also consider any additions and reductions to global capacity.

spectrum, we can place somewhere in the middle companies that have a diverse mix of highly volatile raw materials and companies that have heavy concentration but with a very stable raw material.

The second critical feature for analysis of raw materials risk is the presence or absence of pass-through provisions, or any kind of hedging options in general. If the raw material cost suddenly spikes, impacting the business's COGS, can the company pass the increased cost onto the customer and maintain its margins? If such a contractual provision exists, how is the price calculated? Is it based off a moving average? Does it only apply at a certain threshold?

In sum, it's typically better from a risk perspective to have a diverse set of raw materials. However, even in the presence of resource concentration, the risk can be mitigated through an assessment of the material's volatility and pass-through-ability.

21

CAPITAL INTENSITY

The spectrum of capital intensity refers to a company's dependence upon hard, fixed assets, or PP&E, to generate revenues. On one end of the spectrum, you have capital-intensive firms, and on the other you could place the "capital-lite" firms.

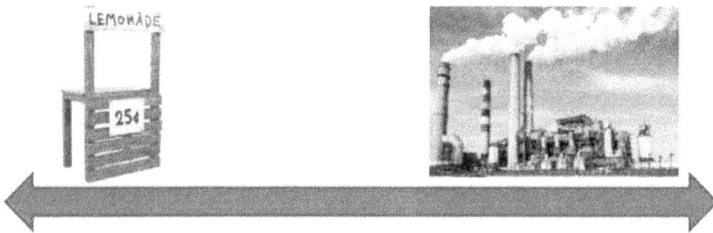

In the former case, images of big factories, manufacturing plants, intermediary facilities, and other infrastructure come to mind. In the latter case, we see "asset light" companies who either outsource the heavy lifting of fixed costs or operate service-focused models.

As an initial observation, one may notice a direct correlation between this spectrum and the general concept of the value chain. Companies found closer to raw materials on the value chain will generally be more capital intensive than the companies that are found closer to the customer.

Quantitatively, the categorization of capital intensity impacts the share of cash outflows attributed to CapEx vs. OpEx. Capital lite firms allocate most of their cash outflows in OpEx, and are the firms more comfortably analyzed through the framework of operating margins (EBITDA). Conversely, for firms with substantial hard assets, it becomes even more important to look at cash flow metrics (like EBITDA less CapEx), given the relative magnitude of CapEx as a source of cash outflows.[41]

At the core of this expenditure mix lies some consideration of cost variability and scalability, which will be covered more in the next section. These factors essentially deal with the degree a company can flex operations, ramping production up and down, while maintaining relatively stable margins. Capital-lite firms can adjust product and service volumes with a fair amount of freedom, as it's more or less about placing smaller/greater amounts of order volumes. A capital-intensive business, on the other hand, is stuck with a material fixed cost base that needs to be covered through contribution margin.

For the purposes of credit analysis, this translates into a trade-off between probability of default and recovery value. A capital-lite firm might have a lower probability of default, all else being equal, because of the relative ease of scaling production up and down and being free from the burden of heavy capital overhead. However, if a bankruptcy

---

[41] You would do well in also separating Maintenance CapEx from Growth CapEx. See the next chapter for more on this.

were to occur, the capital-lite firm will generally produce a lower recovery value than its capitally intensive counterpart. Stated in reverse, a company with hard assets will tend to have greater liquidation value and staying power in the event of an adverse event, but it may have less flexibility in stomaching volatile demand shocks.

From the framework of competitive landscape, it's important to note here that a capitally intense industry will likely have greater barriers to entry. Consider the difficulty in starting a telecommunications company (requiring a physical network spanning multiple geographies) versus a lawn care company selling products and services door-to-door. The cost of new entry (CONE) for the former is in orders of magnitude greater than it is for the latter.

I recommend reading the next two sections as a complement to this one to further solidify the ideas behind capital intensity. To sum up thus far, a capitally intense firm is not necessarily better or worse than its capital-lite counterpart; what's important is to identify the relevant category and know where the divergent areas of focus belong.

22

COST VARIABILITY

In the last chapter we covered capital intensity, which implied some aspect of cost variability. I recommend reading that section in conjunction with this one. Here we will explicitly address the spectrum of fixed and variable costs.[42]

The concept of cost variability directly impacts operating leverage and business scalability. On one end of the spectrum, we have companies with a relatively fixed cost structure and a high degree of operating leverage. Firms toward this end of the spectrum include airlines, software, pharmaceuticals, manufacturers, and others. In each of these cases, there is a high up-front cost (PP&E purchase or build-out, R&D, other CapEx, factory rent, etc.) that is present from the very first unit sold but is essentially non-increasing with subsequent units.

On the other end of the spectrum, we see companies with low operating leverage and a highly variable cost structure. Examples of

---

[42] We consider fixed costs to be those that are fairly steady irrespective of business volumes (costs like rent and salaries), whereas variable costs are those that are directly dependent upon business volumes.

business models here include grocers, whose primary costs are related to merchandise inventory, and consulting firms who charge clients hourly and need minimal office space (as they can work on-site with the clients).

Businesses with high operating leverage have a greater dependency on volumes to generate any profitability. The breakeven level of production will be higher, which translates into a form of risk. However, the advantage of such a dynamic is that the business can benefit from economies of scale, whereby the per-unit cost of production decreases with volumes as the fixed costs get spread over a wider quantity. Ultimately this means that the EBITDA margins can expand with greater production volumes, even if unit pricing remains flat.[43]

It's important to highlight that the concept of cost variability applies to both OpEx and CapEx. In the former case, you would contrast the nature of relatively constant costs like rent, administrative salaries, and other G&A items with that of variable costs like raw materials, direct labor, or other COGS. As a starting point, you could assume that COGS represent variable costs, and SG&A represents fixed costs. However, you'll need to refine this further, as management will often tell you that some SG&A is variable (and, on occasion, COGS contains fixed items like depreciation). For modeling purposes, you can build your SG&A assumption as a percentage of sales (manually increasing/decreasing this percentage depending

---

[43] For those to whom "operating leverage" is a new concept, I recommend googling the topic and viewing graphs of economies of scale. I'm assuming that most readers will already be at least somewhat familiar with it.

on revenue growth each period), you can model SG&A growth as a percentage of sales or as a beta to revenue growth, or you can split your SG&A into separate categories of variable and fixed SG&A, using percentage of sales for the variable portion and manual entries for the fixed portion.

For the case of CapEx, the distinction to keep in mind is Maintenance CapEx vs. Growth CapEx. The first case, which involves maintaining existing equipment (or assets) and replacing it when it becomes obsolete, is a recurring, fixed expenditure. The latter category of Growth CapEx is the acquisition of assets that is directly tied to new revenue growth initiatives and is, hence, a variable (and even discretionary) expenditure.

In sum, which cost structure you find more desirable as an investor will depend upon your objectives, including whether you will be participating as a lender or owner, in addition to your view on the current macroeconomic climate. It is also fair to say that businesses with higher operating leverage should be offset with lower financial leverage, and businesses with lower operating leverage can generally handle more turns of financial leverage.

Finally, on a more academic point, let us also remember that in the long run everything is variable—in other words, how you classify "fixed" or "variable" will largely involve some assumption about a relevant time horizon for operations.

23

LABOR-CAPITAL SPLIT

Aspects of the content here will overlap with that in the prior two sections, but I feel that this topic deserves its own treatise. To what degree is the business in question dependent upon people for producing its solutions as opposed to relying on capital? Is the company people-focused or capital-focused? In a sense, the answer will often correlate with whether the company sells services or products, respectively, though that does not necessarily have to be the case. For background, consider again the Cobb-Douglas equation, which essentially states that all output (products and services) is a function of labor and capital.

On one end of the spectrum, we see people-focused businesses, such as financial advisors, consultants, and direct selling businesses, to name a few. On the other end, we see the capitally intensive production businesses that rely on massive facilities and state-of-the-art technology.[44] Somewhere in the middle we can consider businesses like restaurants or entertainment and other media, which rely on both human performers and physical capital (sets, venues, production equipment, etc.).

Quantitatively, the labor-capital split suggests some aspect of variability, a topic covered in the prior two sections. I would add to this discussion here by outlining a sub-spectrum within labor costs that pits commission-based payments against salaries.

Naturally, commission streams will be more variable than salaries, which have a relatively fixed nature. You could also delineate the "commissions" category into up-front vs. trailing commissions, with the former being more variable than the latter.[45] In the middle, there might be some sort of mix with salaries (fixed) and large bonuses (variable). The more variable the cost base is, the more flexibility the business has in weathering cyclicality. Furthermore, commissions-based businesses may have fewer severance obligations and other on- and offboarding headaches. However, you might achieve marginally lower economies of scale compared to the scenario where a manager can motivate a salaried employee to generate more revenue at the

---

[44] Consult the *Capital Intensity* chapter for more details.

[45] At risk of stating the obvious, salaries are fixed payments independent of volumes, whereas with commissions, "you eat what you kill." Up-front commissions involve an "up-front" payment associated at the time of a transaction; whereas trailing commissions involve "trailing" payments that happen over a contract's life or other defined time period (see annuity or insurance brokers, for example).

same pay level. There may also be more difficulties surrounding hiring and retention in such businesses.

As an illustrative example, consider the direct selling (or multi-level marketing) industry, where individual sellers get hired as "consultants"/"representatives"/"distributors," and so on. These individuals will, traditionally speaking, only get compensated when actual products are sold, or when salespeople they have recruited successfully sell. Yet only the tip-top of performers actually make any livable commissions (hence, the "pyramid" imagery). Consequently, the MLM firms are plagued with high turnover rates (>50% annually) and are faced with a nonstop challenge in motivating their sellers to continue being engaged and evangelize others into the cause. The degree of this administrative effort is not the same for companies who manage salaried employees, as the salaries are generally sufficient for supporting basic lifestyle needs and provide the worker some forward-looking visibility and personal stability, which imbue their own intrinsic motivations.

Among salaries, there is a distinction to be made between low-paying and high-paying roles. Businesses operating with an employee base on the low end are subject to a greater degree of wage pressure risk. Consider a fast-casual restaurant losing already-depressed margin in the face of increasing minimum wages. A $1 increase in the minimum wage can be substantial on a percentage basis. In these cases, it's essential to be familiar with related legislation in the impacted localities, to better understand how these wages will move.

On the high end, businesses start running into key-man risk, or the relative "irreplaceability" of key individuals. Perhaps this is most commonly experienced in boutique consulting or financial advisory practices, or businesses that are branded heavily with the image and ethos of their founders (and potentially becoming cults of personality). In such businesses, it's critical to identify contractual provisions and incentives deployed to address this risk. In other words, how easy is it for the key person to leave the company, and to what degree can they take clients, assets, or other property away with them?

In sum, the union of these last three chapters has covered cost variabilities and some of the idiosyncrasies associated with both labor- and capital-intensive business models. As with many other spectrums, it's not about debating which end is better, but understanding the relative trade-offs, and more importantly, which questions to ask.

24

CAPACITY AND UTILIZATION

For businesses managing physical capital—particularly those for whom the acquisition of such PP&E is both a barrier to entry and a competitive advantage—the concepts of capacity and utilization come to the foreground. What percentage of capacity is the plant running at and how much reserve capacity is available? What is the property's occupancy rate? What is the utilization of the company's equipment?

The spectrum will conceptually plot the possible degrees of utilization, and this will be less about comparing different business models and more about differentiating the merits of running at a high versus low utilization.[46] On one end, we see companies with brand-new assets running at 0% utilization. On the other end, we have companies running at max (100%) capacity. Of course, these endpoints are not

---

[46] How utilization is specifically defined can vary by company and industry, but the percentage is effectively calculated as total current output / total potential output.

equilibria and rarely represent any real-life situations. Most commonly you will see companies operating in the 60s to 80s percentage ranges, however, so we can narrow the range of focus and reframe the spectrum as being one of *underutilization vs. overutilization*.

As an exercise before we continue, consider the power generation, energy, chemicals, leasing, trucking, airline, hotel, and restaurant industries, to name a few. Let's reflect upon how the concept of utilization applies to each, in addition to what "healthy" levels might look like.[47]

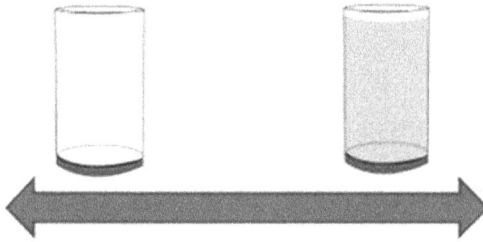

On the side of underutilization (where the company's capacity rate is lower than the industry average), a business can be criticized for not being efficient with its capital and potentially misjudging the level of demand for its product. There may also be greater OpEx required to maintain or store the undeployed fleet or capacity (compared to a right-sized level). However, the benefit of relative underutilization is that there will be a reduced need for Growth CapEx, given that the existing capacity base can absorb near-term demand

---

[47] Consider industry metrics such as capacity factors, rig utilizations, mineral reserves, plant capacities, fleets deployed, passenger miles, and occupancy rates.

growth. This factor can not only bolster a company's near-term cash flow outlook, but also it can provide the company some strategic flexibility in which clients it takes on, given that an up-front CapEx investment for incremental production volumes won't be necessary. Also note that there is a critical difference between an underutilized plant located in a new, growing market versus one found in a saturated, mature market (the latter scenario typically being much worse). In other words, it's nice to have an underutilized plant when you expect new orders to come your way, but it's a headache when it sits there as extra, costly space that is unproductive.

Conversely, when a company's assets are relatively overutilized or near max capacity, it suggests an impending need to build out new capacity to accommodate incremental demand. The large cash outflow associated with such an accommodation is undesirable, particularly if the firm is cash constrained by financial leverage or other factors. Yet, on the other hand, if industry demand is highly visible and expected to continue growing for many subsequent years, taking the hit now can lead to better opportunities and competitive advantages later. It is also worth highlighting that a max capacity operation by definition has no reserves or redundancies. This means the margin for error, in addition to upside optionality, is much smaller, thereby further incentivizing the need to make the expansionary investment.

To summarize, ask yourself how the business's utilization rates compare to those of its competitors, acknowledging the circumstantial factors at play and identifying the relative strategic trade-offs.

The next set of spectrums will be more macro-focused, or "top-down," measuring exposures to broader market conditions.

SOME MACRO THEMES

25

CYCLICALITY

One of the most common categorizations for business models entails the issue of cyclicality, or the sensitivity to economic and business cycles. Cyclicality could be said to measure the degree to which a company's destiny is in its own hands. Is the company generating its own success or is it riding the waves of the wider economy?

The spectrum here goes from hyper-cyclical to countercyclical companies, with non-cyclical companies in the middle.

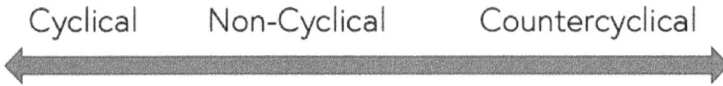

Cyclical   Non-Cyclical   Countercyclical

Cyclical companies will have revenues correlated to the expansion and contraction of the broader economy. Common industry examples include automobiles, housing, and discretionary consumer goods and services.[48] You could also throw in asset managers

---

[48] Consider the example of Callaway Golf, whose financials took a big downswing in the Great Recession, but bounced back during the recovery.

with large equity exposures, who have revenue streams that will necessarily correlate with the stock market. Thirdly, we can point to the kind of cyclicality associated with energy and other commodities, which not only will cycle with the economy but also will have their own sub-market cycles within a given bull or bear market.

A critical feature to assess in a deal with cyclicality is the implied valuation multiple of the transaction. Cyclical companies should largely have lower leverage than the industry average. Too often distressed scenarios occur because a company undertakes "peak cycle" leverage right before the industry heads into a mid- or down cycle.[49] Investing during a down cycle is more or less the ideal (since upside is "guaranteed"), especially when you have tolerance for a longer time horizon. Still, it can be perfectly fine to invest at a peak cycle, provided that the valuation multiple you are investing at is lower than what it would be (or has been) for the company in a mid cycle. Another way to look at it is to calculate the average EBITDA of a company through its economic cycle (adjusting for any secular growth) and base your leverage and valuation metrics on that.

Given that, in a down cycle, revenues can fall off a cliff irrespective of what the cyclical company does, the variability of the business's cost base also becomes an essential consideration. "What levers can management pull?" is the associated line of questioning. Can they eliminate bonuses? Reduce the labor force? Renegotiate

---

[49] For cyclical companies, it's essential to identify what portion of the cycle the company is in. Conceptually, you should visualize a sine wave function, with peaks and troughs, and determine where the company currently sits on the wave.

with suppliers? Sell an underperforming asset? Controlling costs becomes nearly the sole focus for an executive at this stage.

Non-cyclical companies, as the category suggests, are those whose operations are largely immune from the macroeconomic business cycle. Think about consumer staples and other non-discretionary products. Utility companies are a prime example given the non-cyclical demand for electricity (lights, A/C, charging electronics), which should always be present. We can also lump in various essential pharmaceuticals or food products.

Somewhat like non-cyclical companies, you could also consider firms with incredibly strong secular tailwinds, which carry enough momentum to power the company's growth even through the down cycles. Quantitatively speaking, this could look like a growing firm that generates +40% in an upmarket and +2% in a down market. The cyclicality has some impact onto the revenue trajectory, but the secular trend keeps the revenue from heading into sharply negative territory.

To add another flavor to this category, you could even reflect on companies that are non-cyclical with respect to the broader business cycle yet have their own within-industry cyclicality. A classic example of this phenomenon can be found with insurance carriers and the insurance cycle. Insurance premiums begin to fall due to increased competition, when claims and catastrophes are rare, until the industry experiences some material spike in claims and losses accumulate. At that point, the insurance companies would need to raise premiums in order to offset some of the realized losses. The loss-causing factors (severe weather, black swan event, etc.) can often be completely unrelated to the economic cycle.

The third category (and other end of the spectrum) is countercyclical firms. These businesses exhibit a similar volatility to cyclical firms, except in the opposite direction. When the times are bad for most firms, the countercyclical businesses will outperform. You might see auto parts retailers (because a frugal consumer would repair their own car instead of buying a new one), discount grocers, and certain alcohol companies outperform. In the financials sector, I've run into the countercyclical demand of market-makers and restructuring advisory shops. In the former case, these trading firms have seen doubling of profits in times when the markets have experienced drastic shocks, yet they are highly constrained when markets are calm and steady. In the latter case of restructuring situations, think about the demand for lawyers and counsel by companies facing bankruptcy, who will pay a premium for these services.

As a final countercyclical example, you could consider debt collectors or certain real estate firms such as those that run foreclosure auction processes. More defaults could translate into more volumes (and concurrently more revenue) for these kinds of firms.

In the context of a portfolio strategy, the countercyclical companies can make excellent additions. Plus, from a behavioral perspective, they can provide the comforting narrative of: "This company will shine when all the others are falling, and when this one falls, you won't care because all the others are performing strong."

In the context of this discussion, note that the qualitative categories of cyclicality can be depicted quantitatively using beta coefficients. A high beta to the economic cycle implies high cyclicality. A beta of zero indicates non-cyclicality. And a negative beta describes countercyclicality.

In summary, it's important to consider the cyclicality of the business you're looking at, especially as you consider longer-term viability of the business model. Is demand for the company's products or services cyclical? Is the model flexible enough to ride out a variety of macroeconomic waves? How does the cyclicality fit in with the correlations of the rest of the portfolio?

26

GEOGRAPHIC EXPOSURE

Geographic exposure, broken down both in terms of revenue sources and supply chain mix, is another factor to consider. Are the operations and sales of the business concentrated in a particular region or are they spread around?

On one end of this risk spectrum, we put businesses concentrated in one specific region, and on the other extreme we consider multinational firms with footprints that span across the globe.

The concentration-related risks here are similar to those found in the earlier mix and diversification chapters. To gauge the risk found with this flavor of concentration, we should look for material idiosyncrasies within specific locales. What is meaningfully different about the geographies that the company operates in? How do these differences impact our assessment of the firm's performance?

Most commonly, geographic mix relates to risks stemming from weather-related events and political developments affecting a local economy. For example, if a company was selling mostly in Florida, you might think about how the hurricane season, the lack of cold weather, and demographics (high number of retirees, urban vs. rural split, etc.), among other factors, will impact the business. As an example, during the early COVID lockdowns, there was a firm selling hip and knee replacements, whose operations were concentrated in Florida. The cessation of elective surgeries effectively halted the revenues for this company, and the specific timing of Florida's reopening (as opposed to other states) was a critical factor in the liquidity projections.

Another example is a mortgage REIT with commercial real estate in New York City. The value of the investment directly relates to local supply and demand for office space, hotel occupancy, and tourism, *specifically* in New York. Compared to more geographically diversified REITs, this REIT underperformed, given some of the acute headwinds faced in New York.

From a strategic perspective (particularly when it comes to barriers to entry), keep in mind a company's logistical proximity to where the "action" is. The market leader in leasing of mats for energy pipeline projects is located right next to the Permian Basin, where various pipeline projects that need hardwood mats are taking place. This proximity has directly translated into a lower leasing charge to the customer, given the shorter distance (lower fuel costs) associated with the transportation of the mats.

Similarly, a leading sodium cyanide[50] producer intentionally has its plants located near the gold mines (who are, de facto, its customers) in order to reduce the fuel costs behind its commoditized chemical product. Furthermore, the chemical can become unstable

---

[50] Sodium cyanide is used in gold mining to extract the gold from the ore.

if transporting it over long distances, which further emphasizes the value of geographical proximity.

Many large companies and market leaders have already mastered these logistical efficiencies. If not, or in the case of newer companies, it's important to get a sense of how valuable geographical proximity is for competitive advantage.[51]

In any event, you should always have a sense of the geographical exposure of revenue and costs for the business in order to understand the idiosyncratic, regional risks.

---

[51] Phrased alternatively, ask yourself... how important are tight logistics in the considered industry? Is it a point of differentiation for the company? What would the impact of a short-term supply chain disruption be?

27

MARKET FRAGMENTATION

Along the lines of top-down analysis, let's briefly consider the general structures of an existing market. The manner in which the "pie" is divided will inform the attributes and relevant strategies of the business you're analyzing.

On one end of the spectrum, you have highly fragmented markets where there's no clear number one (or where the market leader may have <5% share). Consider markets dominated by small businesses, such as your local dry cleaner or shoe repair shop. Or on a slightly more corporate level, take something like the nutraceuticals or restaurant industries, where any individual brand represents a sliver of the total market.

Typically, high fragmentation has greater risk (but also potentially greater opportunity, if the business can knock out or roll up with other small firms), given that the consumer has indicated some level of indecision and noncommittal behavior. A highly fragmented market suggests that something structural could be preventing any company from achieving scale, or it could simply mean that the market is new. Either way, it behooves you to identify *why* the market is fragmented and whether you expect it to remain as such.

On the other end of the spectrum you have monopolies, with one dominant player to rule them all. In practice, you are more likely to see this setup in ultra niche industries where the incumbent has a unique advantage and where larger conglomerates are disincentivized to break into what would be, from their perspective, a market far too small to be worth pursuing.

From a different lens you could consider a monopolistic situation as one where a company has a patent or proprietary R&D giving them a winner-take-all advantage in a particular vertical (e.g., pharmaceutical companies within specific drug categories). The company may have a sort of "exclusivity" that gives them dominance; it's critical to explore how long their status of "monopoly" is expected to last.

In either case, if the company you are analyzing is effectively in a monopoly (or something close, like being a #1 player with a 60% share, while the rest of the 40% is highly fragmented), that can generally be considered good from a near-term risk perspective, given the high bargaining power. On the other hand, you also want to be mindful of industry disruption risks, as a monopolist's high prices are attractive to new competition compared to the often unpalatable competitive environments in highly fragmented markets.

In the middle of the spectrum we would put in oligopolies, or industries that have a mix of dominant players. Consider the cell phone industry with AT&T, Verizon, and Sprint (and others) or the automobile industry, with Ford, Chevy, and so on. Here it becomes critical to be able to explain the competitive positioning and differentiation of your company *and* that of the other competitors. Barring information limitations, it's important to be able to speak as competently about the oligopoly competitors as you do about the target company. When a consumer makes a decision (or there is an RFP), why do they go with competitors when they reject your company? Or vice versa: For what reason might someone buy your company's solution over the other leading players' solutions?

I would be remiss not to include the fact that markets can be subject to sudden structural changes, causing a drastic shift in equilibria. Consider two examples: the mattress industry and the skincare industry.

The mattress industry was fairly stable, with incumbents Serta Simmons and Tempur Sealy holding a comfortable position of dominance. Then the "mattress-in-a-box" trend disrupted everything, as convenient, sub-$500 mattresses produced overseas proliferated throughout the market. This shift not only dented volumes and pricing of the legacy mattress brands, but it also disrupted the traditional retail channels (see Mattress Firm bankruptcy), compounding the damage.

Somewhat analogously, the skincare and cosmetic industry also had comfortable incumbents until it was overtaken by the power of Instagram influencers and their promotion of indie brands. This relative democratization of advertising combined with accelerating product cycles created distress for legacy players.

The point in these last two examples highlights the commonly given (but perhaps not commonly implemented) advice for legacy incumbents to always stay agile and create the new trends, rather than relying on their coattails of prior success.

As with some other chapters, I'm not including specific guidance or value judgments, as specific situations can vary wildly, but the key starting point for this topic is to consciously identify what the fragmentation of the market is and which forces have been driving that structure. Ask yourself what the market position of the company is and what its pricing power is, and that exploratory frame should lead you to the answers that address these risks.

28

REGULATORY SENSITIVITIES

Every business is subject to a certain degree of regulation, though some are more so than others. A consistent formulation for this section would be to plot out deregulated business models on one end of a spectrum, with hyper-regulated industries on the other.[52] But degree of regulation could be expressed both in terms of the number of jurisdictions in which a business operates (single vs. multiple) and the legal intensity or red tape within such jurisdictions. How to integrate these two variables isn't entirely clear, making a rank-ordering of examples a bit more subjective in this case. Instead, I will highlight below a variety of regulatory flavors.

---

[52] The natural preference will be in favor of business models with lower regulation. Yet a counter thought to this sentiment is that regulation-heavy environments can serve as barriers to entry, but this fact usually isn't enough to offset the undesirable risks posed by regulation.

Sometimes the viability of a business is dependent upon regulatory approval of a particular event. For example, a midstream pipeline operator (and related servicing companies) will face headwinds if the government delays approval of (or outright cancels) its project. Consider the situation surrounding Enbridge's Line 3 pipeline project, and the associated multi-year delays. Another example could be the government's approval of a merger or acquisition. Shortly before this book's writing, there was great uncertainty surrounding the approval of the Sprint and T-Mobile merger, which caused related spreads to widen around telecomm companies and related services. But once the transaction was cleared, risk premia reduced.

Approvals could be manifested in discrete events as addressed above, or they could be a regular part of ongoing business activities, particularly in the example of new product rollouts. Here I provide the example of a publicly traded, multinational ATM manufacturer that sells its equipment to enterprise-level banks with long sales cycles. Given the importance of financial security, the new ATM models have to go through a certification process across various local, regional, and national jurisdictions, in addition to the internal protocols of the sophisticated bank customers. This ATM manufacturer faced certification delays in some international locales, pushing revenues back a few periods and creating entry points for competitors. As an analyst, it would be difficult to predict such delays in advance, but you should be able to identify that the potential for such delays exists more so for this kind of company (whose production process involves overcoming regulatory checkpoints) compared to other business models.

Extending the relevance of international regimes, let's briefly reflect upon the seismic impacts that geopolitical decisions can have. A clear example is the US and China trade war, which showcased heavy tariffs imposed on a variety of goods. US companies with Chinese supply chains saw sharp upticks in their costs of goods, compressing margins and disrupting operations.[53] Shortly after, at the early onset of COVID (during the few weeks when this was only a China problem), US companies with Chinese supply chains took a beating, given that manufacturing workers were staying home, creating delays in order fulfillment.

In a completely different part of the world, investors experienced the significant implications of Brexit and its various postponements. As an example, I diligenced an international real estate brokerage firm that had recently acquired operations in the UK. The announced delays in Brexit created increased uncertainty, which led to a relative pause in commercial real estate decision-making (renewal of leases, negotiations for appropriate pricing, etc.). Such a pause resulted in lower transaction volumes, which translated to lower revenues and profitability for the company, in addition to a dip in the trading price of the related security.

Both this case and the China examples illustrate the importance of being familiar with the regulatory environments of the company's geographies as well as the current events that shape the regulations.

From a non-geopolitical standpoint, consider also impacts from domestic factors, such as minimum wage laws. I have seen such legislation directly impact profitability and security spreads for restaurants

---

[53] Consider the section on raw materials risk again, and the ability to pass through costs onto customers. The economic effects are in ways similar, though the cause here is exogenous, rather than being a result of supply and demand forces.

in the fast-casual and QSR spaces. Other industries would be comparatively immune to minimum wage laws but could face exposure to other restrictions. Knowing which law is relevant to a business often gets learned through experience, but if you can identify the relevant laws before they become topical, you will gain an edge.

Sometimes the laws can be fairly innocuous on the surface but have seismic impacts within a market. When I analyzed power companies, electricity prices in the ERCOT region (~Texas) were very suppressed due to the subsidies given to renewable energy generation. The wind farm operators were able to bid their power at a negative variable margin, driving the aggregate market price down for everyone else and draining the financial health for traditional base load and peaker plants in the area. These subsidies produced a substantial butterfly effect whose cause wasn't immediately obvious to investors until the symptoms multiplied.

Another form of legal risk is the likelihood of a company getting into compliance trouble and facing remedial actions and penalties. One of the leading, publicly traded money transfer and remittance companies experienced both of these impacts. Bad actors were using the platform for money laundering and other scams, so the US government imposed on this company both a financial penalty and a requirement to restructure the workflow of its product. The direct impact of the penalty is obvious.[54] The impact of the required

---

[54] It's worth mentioning that both the size and timing of the payment was changed many times (through negotiation and legal efforts). Each announced modification served as a price event for the stock and serves as a great example of added event risk.

change in protocol was particularly interesting. Prior to the change, customers were, in certain cases, allowed to utilize money transfer services without ID. Furthermore, there were loose quantity minimums. After the US government mandated increased compliance (which led to ID requirement, transaction rules, etc.), a sizable chunk of this company's volumes vanished. The company lost users, not only because these extra requirements created customer experience frictions, but also because the fraudsters moved their laundering activities elsewhere onto other platforms. It turns out that this latter category was quite meaningful; hence the significantly lower transaction volumes for the company. The broader lesson here is that some industries are subject to greater scrutiny and more stringent standards than other industries, and it's important to gradiate between these extremes when considering your specific target company.

As cumbersome as it can be, the regulatory imposition of a financial penalty or compliance requirement is at least somewhat manageable. In other circumstances, the government will outright force a business to shut down.

This existential risk is present, for example, in the MLM / direct selling industry (think about companies like Herbalife or Amway). Specific to this case is the idea that the US government requires such companies to be centered upon products sold rather than the selling of a "start your own business" idea. In other words, the guidelines put in place are meant to prevent pyramid schemes, though the line between legitimate sales organization and scheme can sometimes be blurry. You can read examples of how these companies have fared online. This industry presents an even more extreme case where legal risk is paramount compared to other investments (and why you'll often find—and should expect—a noticeable risk premium in the price of securities for such companies).

On this topic of existential risk, there is also the facet of certain industries "popping" into existence almost overnight, due to the introduction of novel regulation. One example is a financial services trust company dealing with Safe Harbor IRAs. There was legislation that passed in the early 2000s that forced the retirement plan accounts (401(k)s, etc.) of certain terminated employees to be rolled over into Safe Harbor IRAs. The proliferation of this kind of vehicle spurred the creation of new companies that existed solely to manage these Safe Harbor IRA accounts.

Similarly, there have been examples arising from very specific legislation, including the introduction of brokered CDs (certificates of deposit) and changes in the healthcare marketplace. Predicting legal changes in advance can be tricky, but at the very least, your investment thesis should identify which kinds of reasonably likely legal changes could impact the business.

We've covered various aspects pertaining to the influence of the regulatory environment. I would add one more, by highlighting the impact of government budgets. Of course, companies who sell products or services to the government will be at greater risk to changes in how the politicians vote to allocate the budget. For example, I saw the direct step-down in scale for a leading Humvee manufacturer when the US government announced sequestration and a reduction in forces overseas. Few armed conflicts meant few Humvees demanded. In a similar fashion you can see volatility in businesses related to Medicare, Medicaid, and other healthcare legislation. You could gauge aspects of this risk quantitatively by simply measuring what percentage of revenues come from government clients or through government programs.

We can't escape regulatory risk. As demonstrated here, regulatory risk comes in a variety of flavors, and it's important to know which one you're dealing with. Again, it's not really a question of *if* the business has exposure to regulatory risk. But rather, what kind of regulation is it exposed to?

These last couple of spectrums will touch upon some aspects of management strategy and other miscellaneous items.

MISC

29

ORGANIC VS. INORGANIC GROWTH STRATEGY

When considering the growth strategy of a business, a conversation (and spectrum) of organic vs. inorganic growth becomes inevitable. Will a company pay to acquire its customers or draw them in naturally? Will the business purchase a game-changing piece of technology or develop it on its own? Most broadly, will a company take revenue share from existing competitors, or purchase that market share outright through mergers and acquisitions?

This section will focus on this broad, third thrust.

A company's organic growth rate sheds light onto the health of its value proposition, as it's a direct reflection of demand for that company's particular solution. Executing on inorganic growth happens opportunistically, propelling a company further along the race in a shorter amount of time, irrespective of long-term viability.

Risks present in organic growth strategy are effectively encompassed throughout the entire book, since natural revenue growth or decline is the output from all the inputted spectrums. So here we will focus in on inorganic idiosyncrasies, noting that the strategy of acquiring companies can be acute or chronic.

In an acute scenario, we consider examples of large M&A transactions, where we might, for example, see the #2 and #3 players merge to become #1. We also consider less extreme examples, such as where company A buys company B, which is 30% of company A's revenue. The main point is that we are differentiating between these paradigm-shifting business transformations and more innocuous tuck-in or bolt-on acquisitions. Recent acquisitions in the former category are Charles Schwab–TD Ameritrade, Fiserv–First Data, Disney–21st Century Fox, and T-Mobile–Sprint.

In these discrete events, we often see tactical, game theory motivations at play. Laggards combine to catch up to the leader, leaders combine to squash out the mid-size growers, incumbents buy out the hot startups in order to maintain pace on an accelerating treadmill, and so on. Reasons abound and generally center upon market share, technology, and resource considerations.[55]

As an analyst, it can be difficult or impractical to incorporate unannounced transformative M&A transactions into an assessment of a company's risk. Most of the time the separation of wheat and chaff (in terms of analyst quality) comes from understanding and modeling of pro forma business operations and timelines to integrate, adequately sifting through which "synergies" are reasonable as opposed to which are used as overly optimistic addbacks to disguise actual declines in profitability. It is so important that you critically assess the credibility of each synergy line item.

Issues surrounding this kind of M&A have been covered extensively and in more depth in other literature, so I would encourage the reader to independently pursue that path further, if desirable. For the remainder of this section, we'll focus on the inorganic growth that's persistent and part of the company's going concern.

When we think about businesses growing, our default mindset is to expect organic growth based on the business's own merits. The company sells more products and services (perhaps at higher prices), by attracting more attention and conversion. However, in certain industries, consolidation and "roll-up" strategies become key to near-term growth and success. To illustrate, consider deals present in the insurance brokerage, payments, and dental industries.

---

[55] I would point to the typical distinction of "horizontal" vs. "vertical" integration as another cross section to ponder, but I don't want to deflect too much away from the main point at hand.

Most insurance verticals are highly fragmented—in your mind you may recall interacting with the independent local branch, as opposed to a giant corporate conglomerate. Many of the large private equity-backed companies in the insurance brokerage industry are the result of piecemeal, roll-up strategies where hundreds of small independent businesses are purchased and amalgamated under one corporate umbrella. You can see similar behavior in dental office buyouts, or merchant acquirer residual and portfolio buyouts. These roll-up strategies are the norm rather than the exception.

As an analyst, your main consideration here is to compare the acquisition multiples ("tuck-in" or "bolt-on" multiples) to the valuation multiple of the parent company, to comparable transactions in the current market, and to a historical trend of the company's tuck-in acquisitions. You want to see if these acquisitions are bought at a discount or premium. For example, one could say, all else being equal, if a company valued at 7x EBITDA makes a bolt-on acquisition at 4x EBITDA, that is a favorable outcome, given the arbitrage achieved. In other words, every $4 of acquired value turns into $7 of value once integrated into the parent company. It's effectively buying an asset at 4 and selling at 7. Granted, part of this spread is attributed to the scale differentials of the companies, but the general idea holds.

Say that our 7x EV/EBITDA company keeps making acquisitions, but the multiples of recent tuck-ins have been trending toward 5x or 6x. That should raise a flag in your mind as to why the spread is converging. Perhaps the size of the recent acquisitions was greater. Maybe the market has been tightening due to increased competition or a change in the macroeconomy. You should also consider the financing of the tuck-ins, and whether pro forma leverage for the parent company is increasing or decreasing.

Outside of these generic roll-up strategies, you can see the option of inorganic growth expressed alternatively in other industries. Common situations include a restaurant's decision to buy out existing franchises vs. opening a new store, a telco operator purchasing a competitor's wirelines vs. building out a fresh set, or an infrastructure manager choosing to launch a greenfield vs. brownfield project. These decisions fall under the organic vs. inorganic growth framework, and you should take a stance regarding which kind of growth strategy would benefit the company you are analyzing.

In sum, determine whether acquisitions are an essential part of the management's growth strategy, noting whether such transactions are acute or chronic. And compare the multiples both cross-sectionally and temporaneously, while monitoring the impacts to capital structure and identifying any attempts at masking true business performance through the illusion of synergies.

30

CROSS-SELLING AND INTEGRATION OF BUSINESS LINES

When a business has multiple products or services, the strategy of cross-selling becomes a key consideration. The ability to successfully cross-sell depends on how relatable the different products are (or how relatable they can be marketed to be). A greater ability to cross-sell implies a revenue growth path with less friction or a lower customer acquisition cost compared to the alternative. However, as discussed in the *Business Diversification* section, if the business lines are too related, it can lead to revenue volatility. In other words, an opportunity to gain revenue more easily is often accompanied with the adverse consequence of more easily losing that revenue when there are headwinds.

The spectrum here involves cross-sellability, and the point is to encourage awareness of how the company under analysis utilizes existing opportunities to pursue incremental paths of monetization. On one end of the spectrum, we have companies deploying a high level of cross-selling activities, with the opposite case on the other.

For high cross-selling, consider businesses that sell a core product alongside related accessories. The sale of accessories is directly tied to core product sales; for example, no one will buy a cell phone case if there is no cell phone. Taken a step further, consider businesses that fall under the "razor-razorblade" model, whereby the primary product is offered at an accessible entry point (razor) and profits are generated through accessory replacements (razorblades). In other words, such businesses become about selling as many high-margin "razorblades" as possible while using the sale of the "razor" as a vehicle to get the customer committed to your brand. Such strategy has also been implemented when new hardware technologies race to acquire next-gen market share. This is what happened during the advent of CD, DVD, and Blu-ray players, as manufacturers were willing to sacrifice profits on the media player in order to encourage broad adoption of their platform and recoup value from the disc sales.[56]

Another cross-selling strategy entails distribution of complex products and then selling of value-add services on top of that. Many IT vendors and digital transformation companies will resell commodity technology and then overlay higher margin professional services, making the final package feel specialized. In such cases it's important to distinguish what proportion of that company's demand is driven by the product sale as opposed to the sale of "value-add" services.

---

[56] This can dovetail into a broader conversation about network effects and winner-take-all/most markets.

On the other end of the spectrum, we have companies whose products are completely unrelated and unlikely to be sold together under a bundle. We would see multi-business line conglomerates here, as we did in the section on *Business Diversification*. Rather than re-tread the same ground, I would encourage you to reference that chapter, though I will add an incremental observation here: In the context of cross-selling, having completely unrelated product lines does impede the reduction of customer acquisition cost (since the business is less able to recognize the lower CAC that typically comes from cross- and up-selling).

While cross-sellability on its own doesn't necessarily push us in either direction of risk, its effects and related business growth strategy should be acknowledged in the context of qualitative due diligence.

31

A FEW OTHERS

We could keep slicing risk into different spectrums, but at some point, we'll get meaningfully diminishing returns. If you have experience in machine learning or statistics, this is like the phenomena of whether to keep incorporating additional variables into the regression or deciding that the current set of factors are sufficient to explain the majority of the variance in outcomes.

For this section I will briefly hit on a few other points that don't necessarily need their own chapters, but still merit a mention. We don't have to think about these in terms of spectrums, but rather general patterns and classifications to look out for.

When aggregating all of the individual risk spectrums, it can be helpful to consolidate the insights into a broader narrative arc and/or use familiar terminology that succinctly captures many of the risks. Here are some examples:

THE MELTING ICE CUBE

Businesses that have a stable yet slowly declining top line (perhaps due to technological obsolescence), such as a coin processing or paper shredding company, could be classified as such. When one uses the term "melting ice cube," it implicitly suggests that the company has visible and contracted revenues but with a fairly certain path of gradual attrition.

INFLECTION POINTS

If a business you're analyzing is expected to enter a materially different stage of growth, you would do well to talk about it in terms of an "inflection point." One example I encountered was a telco business with declining 3G revenues, which were on a path to eventually be offset by growing 4G and 5G revenue streams. In other words, the aggregate top line was declining, but on a path to eventually hit an *inflection* point as the newer business (and its positive growth) ends up representing the majority share of that company's revenues, as the scale differentials between the business lines converge.

WHAT DOES THIS COMPANY DO?

RELIANCE ON PASSIVE OR UNINFORMED CUSTOMERS

Some businesses generate profitability only because a material portion of revenue comes from phenomena such as breakage. For example, in a loyalty points program, ~15% of points go unused by the customer. This lack of redemptions directly creates margin through lower costs. Yet if redemptions spiked and the company was forced to provide the rewards (i.e., make purchases), profitability would quickly erode. This breakage phenomenon is also what happens when gym memberships or other subscription memberships go unused.

A similar effect occurs in fintech companies that rely on cash sweep revenue. In other words, the company will make a spread when the client keeps their money uninvested (in cash). For example, this is present in essentially all of the retail trading platforms, in addition to the private wealth managers and independent broker dealers. I've also seen this in a trust business that manages a departing employee's retirement funds until the employee transfers them over at a new employer.

ASSET COVERAGE VS. CASH FLOW

Consider the risk profile of two different kinds of companies. The first is an asset-light services company generating substantial cash flow, for the time being. The second is a production company that utilizes a variety of long-term assets (factory, heavy equipment, and machinery) but is generating near breakeven cash flow. In the former scenario, a lender would want the company to sweep excess cash flow to pay off the debt while profitability remains high. In the latter scenario, a debtholder could be comfortable with little-to-no cash flow because the value of the heavy assets would be sufficient to cover the size of the debt in the event of bankruptcy and a distressed asset sale.

MANAGEMENT CREDIBILITY AND INFORMATION DISCLOSURE

It's important to get a sense of whether management delivers on their projections and is transparent about what has been happening with the business. In other words, one should gauge the degrees of credibility and information disclosure. Investors are often happy to forgive some company underperformance when management is forthcoming with key performance metrics and their characterization of the industry. Conversely, if the management team or PE sponsor holds their cards close to the chest, sharing only what is legally necessary, investors will act more punitively.[57]

One could also characterize this as a "show me" vs. "tell me" situation. For example, if management keeps making excuses for

---

[57] After all, having less information disclosed leads to greater uncertainty, which leads to a higher risk premium and therefore a lower security price, all else being equal.

operational delays, then their words lose credibility, and investors could take the stance of "I'll believe it when I see it," discounting any positive proclamations of the company. Under such a scenario, the security price should be comparatively less sensitive to statements made by management.[58] In the "tell me" situation, investors may be angsty for a silent management team to give color on the company, whether for the purposes of direct analysis that they can apply to their investment decision, or for analogous insights onto competitors and the industry at large.

As with estimates of an asset's fair value, assessing the credibility and transparency of management is best done in conjunction with an estimate of how the market is currently perceiving that credibility and transparency. Then one can incorporate an opinion on whether the market is under- or over-valuating management's words.

SYNERGY PLAY

Despite some late-stage businesses lacking cash flow, they could still represent interesting investment opportunities. A common idea is to

---

[58] In certain distressed asset circumstances, there can manifest a "numbness" of sorts to bad information and disappointment. I encountered one company that reported struggling results for 3 years, despite management reassuring everyone that "we expect cash flow to improve over the next two quarters." At first the disappointments would cause drops in the asset price each time they said this. But eventually, the disappointments failed to move the market, because the market had already priced in the fact that management's assurances were essentially worthless.

invest as a part of a large M&A or LBO where the acquiring management team or the PE sponsor identifies cost savings that can be generated through initiatives like redundancy eliminations, supply chain renegotiations, and other economies of experience and scale. When the pro forma company is sufficiently large, these "synergies" can be very substantial. An analyst's role here is to determine how credible management's estimates of synergies are and to appropriately discount them.[59]

TRANSACTION TYPES

In addition to the fundamentals of the company, it's important to assess the qualities of the deal and transaction itself. Is money coming in, through a debt or equity raise? If so, what will it be used for? Or is money going out via a dividend recap? If a company is being spun out of a larger conglomerate, why is the conglomerate selling? All else being equal, an investor should demand a higher premium for cash-out transactions given the risk of adverse selection.[60]

---

[59] Ideally, one should evaluate these synergies one line item at a time. If this isn't feasible, an aggregate haircut of 15–20% is a reasonable rule of thumb to start with.

[60] In other words, there is an inherent informational asymmetry as the seller may know about an undesirable feature of the asset being sold ("If the company you are selling to me is so great, why are you cashing out?"). Of course, there are innocuous reasons for selling as well, such as an owner's personal desire for liquidity, though these circumstances should also be explored.

32

BONUS CHECKLIST

I've outlined the kinds of risk principles that should cover 95% of diligence efforts. As you've seen, these spectrums aren't the answers themselves, but rather the tools you can use to structure your due diligence.

As a bonus, consider the following structured approach of asking questions and how the spectrums can be applied to it. I've put them in a sequence, but most of the steps can be taken in any order.

Step 1: What problem(s) is the company attempting to solve?
    a. Answer this in the context of the entire value chain.

Step 2: For whom is the company solving it for?
    a. Describe the customers in light of the end market, enterprise/SMB, and other spectrums.

Step 3: What's in it for the company? How badly does the customer want their solution?

    a. What are the terms of its typical commercial transactions and its unit-level economics?

Step 4: Who else is solving this problem?

    a. Assess the competitive landscape.

Step 5: What is (or will there soon be) another way to solve this problem?

    a. Gauge the available substitutes and the potential for technological disruption.

Step 6: How is the company uniquely addressing this problem? What is different about its solution?

    a. Look for competitive advantage and differentiation, both in contrast with other businesses and with substitute offerings.

Step 7: How easy is it to replicate the company's solution?

    a. Consider barriers to entry, whether they are based on capital requirements, regulatory burden, network effects, or other factors.

Step 8: How is the company able to provide its solution? How is it produced and delivered?

    a. This should encompass an analysis of the supply chain and employee base, with its quality and bargaining power.

ACKNOWLEDGEMENTS

I have many different aspirations and projects that I want to work on. I want to acknowledge Kelly for always supporting my endeavors, varied as they are.

And I thank God for guiding me when I don't know where to go next. This handbook's draft had been sitting unopened on my laptop for a few years. Yet in these last weeks leading up to publication, I began encountering "nudges" during prayer, so here we are...

ABOUT
THE AUTHOR

Drago Dimitrov has professionally invested in leveraged loans, high yield bonds, public and private equities, and venture capital. He is a CFA® charterholder and received his MBA from the University of Chicago Booth School of Business.

Website: drago.life
LinkedIn: linkedin.com/in/dragodimitrov
ETH: dragodimitrov.eth

www.ingramcontent.com/pod-product-compliance
Lightning Source LLC
Chambersburg PA
CBHW040923210326
41597CB00030B/5157